The Making of a Black Mayor

A Study of Campaign Organization, Strategies and Techniques in Prichard, Alabama

By John Dean

Joint Center for Political Studies

Designed and printed by Graphics 4, Annandale, Virginia

85-4650

ii

Foreword

From time to time, the Joint Center studies what went right or wrong in a particular election involving minority group candidates. The purpose of such post-mortems is two-fold: to provide an historical perspective and to amass information which might be useful to future political candidates, as well as to the public. One such study was entitled "Baltimore's Failure to Elect a Black Mayor in 1971." Written by Morgan State College Professor G. James Fleming, this study analyzes the candidates, issues, strategies and votes in the September 14, 1971, primary election and gives the author's views on why Baltimore failed to elect a black mayor.

In the present study, we have a post-mortem of the successful bid of Algernon (Jay) Cooper, Jr., to become mayor of Prichard, Alabama. Specifically, it is a detailed account of the successful ingredients — organization, strategies and techniques — of the campaign developed for Cooper.

Author John Dean, a veteran political campaigner, served as Cooper's campaign manager. His report is the definitive account of how he organized the campaign and how Mayor Cooper won. In addition, it is a moving and revealing study of race relations in a small southern town, of black attitudes towards politics and of the political savvy of a seasoned political strategist and a 28-year-old southern-born, northern-educated black lawyer.

Major newspapers and magazines have attempted to take stock of Jay Cooper — the man — who won against great odds. John Dean, who lived and worked with Cooper through the most critical period of his political ordeal, has set his sight on only one aspect of the man, namely, his good fortune in forging, with the decisive help of local and national friends, a sound campaign organization which was capable of beating "the system" with its own methods.

Whether or not Jay Cooper represents the so-called "new black politician," the campaign embodied wisdom and skill, uncanny resourcefulness, tough-minded decisions, the spirit of healthy compromise and a single-minded determination to maintain focus on the only ball in the game. Consequently, the reader, whether student, citizen, office-holder or would-be office-holder has much to learn from this account of the Cooper campaign.

Because of his unique victory, his personality and his ability, not to mention the hard jobs ahead of him as mayor of Prichard, Jay Cooper, like Stokes, Hatcher and Gibson, among others before him, is fast becoming a national figure. His name is not yet a household word, but if his administration shows the kind of skill, pragmatism and sensitivity that went into his campaign, we haven't heard the last of him.

Eddie N. Williams
President

Author's Note:

This study is my personal view of the organization, strategies and techniques I employed in the successful campaign of "Jay" Cooper. It covers the period of my presence in Prichard near the end of the general election campaign, from July 30 to August 8, and for most of the run-off campaign, from August 14 to September 12.

The Joint Center for Political Studies, sponsored by Howard University and the Metropolitan Applied Research Center, is a private, non-profit organization funded by the Ford Foundation to provide research, education, technical assistance and information for the nation's minority elected officials on a non-partisan basis.

TABLE OF CONTENTS

I. INTRODUCTION

Prichard: Social and Political Background

Prichard is the seventh largest city in Alabama. It has a population of 41,578, of which 51 percent is black. It is just north of the city of Mobile in Mobile County. The relative poverty of Prichard in contrast to Mobile, which surrounds it on three sides, is obvious upon entering the city limits. Unemployment, particularly in the black community, is high and housing conditions are as bad as any in the South. Although demographically defined as urban, Prichard is in reality a rural community in appearance, custom and outlook. As with many old and fairly stable Southern communities, its residents are interrelated through marriage, and suspicious of all who are not natives. Prichard is very conservative in philosophy and life style, and looks with some disfavor upon political liberalism and the new youth culture. It had become the custom for Gov. George Wallace to deliver his Labor Day address in Prichard, his stronghold.

The Election

Every four years, Prichard elects a mayor and the five members of its city council in an at-large, non-partisan election. In the August 8, 1972 general election, A. "Jay" Cooper, a black candidate for mayor, received 3,587 votes to 1,763 votes for the white incumbent V. O. Capps. Over 7,646 votes were cast in the largest voter turnout in the history of the city. Jay Cooper received the largest number of votes ever given a black man running for elective office in Prichard and the largest vote ever given a black candidate for mayor of a major Alabama city. In a field of six white candidates, including the 12-year incumbent, he received over 45 percent of the vote.

Cooper's failure to get a majority of the vote made a run-off election necessary and it was held on September 12th. In that election another record was set. Voter turnout increased by 25 percent, with a surprising 10,658 voters going to the polls. A. "Jay" Cooper was elected mayor by 5,601 votes to 5,057 for his opponent. When he was inaugurated on October 2, 1972, Cooper became the first black man since Reconstruction to defeat a white incumbent for mayor in a major Alabama city, and he and John Langham, a black candidate for city council, became the first black men elected to public office in the history of Prichard.

1

The Candidacy of "Jay" Cooper

Algernon Johnson Cooper was born in Mobile, Alabama. He attended the University of Notre Dame where he participated extensively in student, political and community affairs, both on and off campus. Cooper graduated from Notre Dame in 1966 and continued such activities at the New York University School of Law where he helped found the National Black American Law Students Association and was national treasurer of the Law Student Division of the American Bar Association. He graduated from law school in 1969.

While in New York, Cooper also worked for the NAACP Legal Defense Fund and in 1968 was a member of Senator Robert F. Kennedy's campaign staff. When Jay returned to Alabama in 1969, he set up a law office and immediately became involved in civil rights and community activities.

Almost a year before the general election, on August 14, 1971, flanked by Manhattan Borough President Percy Sutton and Atlanta's Vice Mayor Maynard Jackson, Jay Cooper announced his candidacy on the steps of Prichard's City Hall. His announcement was a challenge to the established order in Prichard. White political leaders viewed it as another vain and rather humorous attempt at black political action and were confident that it would founder as had such efforts in the past. They did not believe any black person had sufficient knowledge of political campaigning to pose a serious threat.

There also were reactions from some of the older, more established black leaders in the community. These leaders had developed political accommodations over the years with the power structure of the city and they viewed Cooper's candidacy as a direct and presumptuous threat to their status. They, too, doubted the present level of black political sophistication, and did not believe any black man could beat the incumbent mayor. These leaders also held to the tradition, still prevalent in much of the South, that the mantle of leadership is attained only with age and they were suspicious of this 28 year-old black lawyer, who had returned to Prichard after studying in the North.

Black Political Involvement

Cooper's announcement marked the beginning of political awareness in a black community which had no real history of organized political action. In 1964, C. C. Suggs, Andrew R. Ray and Thomas McAboy had run unsuccessfully for city council. In 1968, C. C. Suggs ran for mayor and John Pogue, Fred Lee Harris and

Thomas McAboy ran for city council. All of these efforts were basically one-man operations, and none of the candidates received more than 1,700 votes. Their campaigns involved speaking to whatever black audiences they could find in the city.

Excluding the NAACP, there were no local black social action organizations which could be converted into political action mechanisms for those campaigns. In addition, no political organizations or core of individual political activists had developed out of those campaigns to serve as a continuing repository of the few political lessons learned. Basically, those efforts had left the black community in Prichard as it had always been: a community of great voter apathy where generations of oppression and intimidation had left their now classic mark. Politics was the business of white folks and if black people voted at all, they voted for the white candidates they were told to vote for or they voted for white candidates because they thought they should.

II. GENERAL CAMPAIGN PLANNING

As he had promised on the steps of city hall, Cooper prepared "an extensive platform for the rehabilitation of Prichard." He operated for the better part of the campaign year with few resources and only a handful of dedicated volunteers and community leaders. Cooper had already developed an unusually effective publicity effort out of his platform themes. Handbills, billboards and media ads incorporating those themes were put into use. The candidate had secured three store-front campaign sites and literature distribution and phone bank activities were in operation at two of them. Some demographic data had been compiled and a voter registration drive had just concluded with the placement of 1500 new black voters on the books.

These efforts had been accomplished even though Cooper had to perform the burdensome task of being both candidate and campaign manager. He had pushed his few community leaders and hard-core of volunteers to the limit of their current abilities in carrying out these activities and they had performed far better than might reasonably have been expected.

The candidate recognized, however, the improbability of victory unless a more cohesive and complete campaign structure could be developed and supervised by experienced political activists. Cooper called upon a few friends in Washington, New York, Ohio, and as far away as Minnesota to volunteer their time to put together the necessary campaign organization. These professionals in turn called some of their friends and by July 30, 1972, ten days before the general election, the campaign manager and other staff began to arrive.

Marathon campaign planning sessions began that evening to assess what was known about the community, what had and had not been done up to that point and to determine what was needed before the election. The sessions revealed that there was an immediate need for more demographic data. Staff would be directed to conduct the necessary research to obtain this data in addition to their other duties, since there was neither time nor personnel to set up a regular research unit.

4

Demographics and Voter Information

An analysis of the available demographic data revealed that of Prichard's population of 41,578, over 21,005 or 51 percent were black. In 1960 the city's population was 47,371 but there had been an out-migration of over 5,793 persons, mainly whites, to Mobile and surrounding townships because of Prichard's general economic decline. The city was $121,000 in debt and over 60 percent of all residents lived in substandard housing. When the dwellings were analyzed by owner and renter occupancy, household income in 84.8 percent of owner-occupied housing, and 99.3 percent of renter-occupied housing was less than $7,500. Over 40 percent of all black families were below the poverty level, and 52.5 percent of all families were on welfare.

Prichard's voting unit is a ward, and there are six wards. Staff was directed to collect the necessary data and draw a map which showed the percentage of black population by ward using a color key (Maps #1 & 2). The map revealed the following characteristics of neighborhoods within each ward:

Black Percentage of Ward Population

Wards........	1	2	3	4	5	6
% Black......	20%-50%	50%-100%	50%-100%	20%-35%	0%	0%

Past Voting and Registration Data

Staff was directed to research the 1964 and 1968 elections for mayor of Prichard. This research revealed that there had been a run-off in the 1964 mayor's race, but no breakdown of the vote by ward was available. The vote totals for the general election and the run-off were as follows:

Total Vote Received by Mayoralty Candidates in the General Election, August 31, 1964

	Vote	%
V. O. Capps....................	2,150	40.4
M. N. Dismuts..............	783	14.7
Luman L. Drew............	1,177	22.1
Cecil M. Rambo............	1,215	22.8
Total..................	5,325	100.00

Total Vote Received by Mayoralty Candidates in the Run-off Election, September 17, 1964

	Vote	%
V. O. Capps	3,514	61.4
Cecil Rambo	2,204	38.6
Total	5,718	100.00

The significance of these two races appears in the run-off. Not only did the vote swing fairly decisively to Capps, but there was an actual increase in voter turn-out.

Because more data was available for the 1968 election and because this was also the first race in Prichard in which a black man, C. C. Suggs, was a candidate for mayor, it provided the Cooper campaign with some idea of ward performance with a racially mixed field of candidates. V. O. Capps won that election without a run-off. The vote by ward was as follows:

Total Vote Received by Mayoralty Candidates in the General Election, August 13, 1968

Wards	1	2	3	4	5	6	A*	Candidates Totals	%
V. O. Capps	663	839	428	889	566	170	5	3,560	52.5
D. T. Davis	334	399	145	171	122	34	2	1,207	17.8
C. S. Dixon	97	284	159	46	41	3	0	630	9.3
N. W. Patrick	38	44	34	9	4	0	0	129	1.9
C. C. Suggs, Sr.	80	689	369	116	2	2	0	1,258	18.5
Ward Totals	1,212	2,255	1,135	1,231	735	209	7	6,784	100.00

*Absentee ballots.

Analysis of this data revealed that Capps swept the thinly populated, but all-white wards #5 and #6. He showed good strength in his own ward #4, getting two-thirds of the vote and just over half of the vote in racially-mixed ward #1. He got about 40 percent of the vote in heavily black wards #2 and #3. Suggs came in second, but probably would have done worse if the field had not been so large. He showed good strength in getting around 30 percent of the vote in wards #2 and #3.

The campaign staff reasoned that Cooper would need over 4,000 votes to win in the general election. He would have to carry wards #2 and #3 as heavily as possible, and come as close to the incumbent as he could in wards #1 and #4 in accumulating that vote.

When Jay Cooper announced his candidacy in 1971, there were only 13,800 registered voters in Prichard, about 6,000 black and 7,800 white. By August 8th, 1972, there were almost 2,000 new voters, 1,500 added by Cooper's registration drive. Staff was directed to determine the distribution of the new vote by ward to be sure the projections for wards #1, 2, 3 and 4 were still viable. The analysis of the 8,300 white and 7,500 black voters showed the following:

Wards	1	2	3	4	5	6	
Totals	2,434	5,274	3,497	2,449	1,461	464	15,811

After the general election, county election officials ruled there could be additional registration from August 19th up to run-off election day on September 12th. A new voter registration drive was organized by the Cooper campaign with a goal of registering at least another 1,000 black voters. By September 12th about 2,000 new voters had been registered with over 1,300 of them having been taken to the registrar's office by the Cooper campaign staff. Thus from August, 1971, to the run-off election in September, 1972, almost 4,000 new voters had been added. This brought the new total to 17,811. The Cooper campaign had added 2,800 black voters to increase their total strength to 8,800 by September 12th.

Polling

A poll was conducted during the general election campaign using a scientifically-developed sample of 400 residents of Prichard of all races, income levels and educational backgrounds. The object was to make a fairly simple determination of the strength of the candidate at that point, although other questions related to local and national issues and to the local and national elections. Results, though not tabulated in any systematic manner, revealed that economic issues on the local and national level were the main concern of the voters. Results also showed that at the presidential level, 27 percent favored McGovern, 24 percent favored Wallace and 17 percent favored Nixon. Cooper led the field of local candidates with a clear majority. (Exhibit #1).

III. BASIC CAMPAIGN STRATEGY; GENERAL ELECTION

Political Premises of the Campaign

Campaign strategy shortly before the general election grew out of a number of carefully reasoned assessments of the incumbent and the physical, social, economic and political conditions of the community. These assessments were gathered from discussions with the candidate and knowledgeable community leaders. They were formulated into the strategies which directed all the themes, approaches and activities of the campaign from that point forward.

During the general election period, the key premise about the general public was that a substantial portion of them, both black and white, were aware of and dissatisfied with the ineptness and mismanagement of Mayor Capps' 12–year administration. There was general recognition that under Capps there had been a steady economic decline and a loss of jobs and residents to more viable parts of Mobile County. Now the city was deeply in debt. Influence peddling in place of the normal delivery of city services was a commonly talked of practice. It was felt that the public sensed some unwillingness or inability of the city administration to attract to Prichard a fair share of federal programs and new industry. The voters wanted a change.

Black Community

In the black community, it was reasoned that general voter apathy born of oppression and intimidation would make a large voter turnout difficult to achieve. This was reinforced by the fact that politics had never touched the average black voter in his own neighborhood and the white Southern media had isolated him from the mainstream of current black political thought and progress. It was understood that many of the established black leaders would do little to remedy this situation because of their perception of Cooper as a threat to their status, even though overtures would continue to be made to them. This situation would in turn make recruitment of a substantial number of volunteers very difficult and thus increase the burden upon senior campaign staff.

In terms of issues, there was some feeling in the community about the particularly bad conditions in black neighborhoods and an understanding of the almost inevitable loss of their educated young black people to areas which offered better job opportunities. Since the death of an old black man while waiting in one of the long food stamp lines, the matter of food stamp distribution had become an emotionally-charged issue. Finally, the campaign felt that a large segment of the black community simply did not believe that black people could mount an effective campaign to win against a white man in Prichard.

White Community

It was expected that there would not be a substantial white vote for Jay Cooper. The assumption was that the candidate might possibly get as much as 10 percent of that vote based on the appeal of his program to their economic self-interest. Many of those who might vote for him in the white community would do so not knowing he was black. Among the larger segment of white voters who did know who Cooper was, it was reasoned that they were certain no black man could become mayor. In the absence of any provocative actions or statements by the campaign they could be expected in their confidence to stay home in large numbers.

The Incumbent

The incumbent mayor would in all probability follow the example of Wallace's new politics in Alabama and not mount an obviously racist campaign against Cooper. It was felt that V. O. Capps would assess the black voter in much the same manner as the Cooper campaign assessed the white voter. He was not expected to allow any provocative action on his part to arouse the black community into a large turnout. Having some sense of his unpopularity among all voters, he would generally maintain a very low profile and let white racism, black apathy and the political incompetence of his opponent's black organization assure him another term.

General Campaign Themes and Approaches

From these premises grew a number of themes and strategic approaches. The central themes of the campaign related directly to the public's general discontent with Capps and to the condition of the city. These themes were that Jay Cooper cared about all of the citizens of Prichard and would help the voters "save" Prichard from its ultimate decline as a livable city. He would rehabilitate the city, bring competence to local government, expand social services, improve law enforcement and end the city's debt. Great emphasis was placed on the candidate's ability to bring in outside resources and increase employment opportunities.

9

The campaign would stay on high ground, and the positive themes of "Save Prichard" would run through all public and media statements and appear in all campaign literature. These themes would be the rationale for the selection of all campaign events and activities.

Black Community

The "Save Prichard" themes were woven into the approach to the black community with emphasis on neighborhood and social services improvements and more jobs. To attack the problems of black voter apathy and political isolation, a strategy of high visibility particularly in wards #2 and #3, with a strong attempt at citizen involvement was adopted. As many meetings with religious leaders, church visits and church functions built around campaign projects were planned as time would permit in order to reach the vast church constituency in this very religous community. Contrary to the limited black campaign efforts of Prichard's past, all of Cooper's activities would be scheduled with a view toward allowing him to touch as many ordinary black citizens as possible, on occasions which dramatized some social issue or campaign theme.

The themes of most interest to black audiences would be used heavily every day on black-oriented radio stations and in the black press. Campaign literature would be distributed continuously in the community during the last days of the election and the phone bank would blanket the neighborhoods repeatedly with requests to register, to vote, to canvass friends and to volunteer in the campaign.

White Community

The premises regarding the white community required a slightly different approach. The "Save Prichard" themes were the same but special emphasis would be placed on improving the economic viability of the city. It would be stressed that Cooper possessed the skills to bring in outside funds and resources. Messages were developed which emphasized these points for limited white newspaper ads and radio spots. The same messages also were included in selected pieces of campaign literature for distribution in white neighborhoods.

The campaign would also make a deliberate effort not to become too black in orientation or message and efforts would be made to recruit local white volunteers to work in their community. The candidate would maintain a low profile in the white community to decrease any further public recognition of him and to reduce any perception on that community's part of the vigor of the campaign.

The Incumbent

The approach to Capps would be to maintain a basically high-ground stance. An attack on him directly, regardless of its validity, would arouse white voters at that point and blow the campaign's cover among those who did not know Cooper was black. This approach also was not necessary because the campaign was extremely confident that its themes incorporated the felt needs of all the citizens. The contrast between the credible and reasonably attainable goals outlined for the city by Cooper and the reality of the city's condition made attack strategies useless at that time.

Campaign Publicity

Possibly better than anything else, the campaign's publicity materials illustrate the wedding of strategy to end-product. The themes were first spelled out along with many other ideas and program proposals in the platform formulated by Jay Cooper in the campaign's early days. During the last weeks before the general election they were refined into a number of precise points. These points, mentioned in general terms earlier, were that the voters should unite with Cooper who was the only candidate qualified to save the city of Prichard. The urgent problems confronting the city were outlined: lack of jobs, poor housing, lack of recreational facilities, unpaved streets, open drainage ditches, a large debt, a corrupt administration, weak law enforcement, long food stamp lines.

Jay Cooper would bring honesty and efficiency to government. He would also bring in federal programs and private industry and begin to address the city's needs systematically to make Prichard a place for all its citizens to live and work with pride.

This message with variations was printed on five different types of handbills, bumper stickers and posters. The language on the handbills also became the basic text of the spots on black and white-oriented radio stations and of the copy for the newspaper ads. It was reduced to classic simplicity: "Save Prichard—Elect Cooper." This message was printed on three outdoor billboards, three flashing electric signs at key intersections and on thousands of lapel stickers (Exhibits #2 through #7).

Because of extremely limited resources, ways were constantly sought to do things or acquire materials without cost to the campaign. After the literature was designed, Cooper asked friends in

Washington, New York and Ohio to provide specific amounts of literature printed at facilities they had access to as a campaign contribution and ship it to Prichard. In this fashion, over 60,000 pieces of literature were produced at no cost to the candidate and in many instances at little or no cost to the contributors.

Fund Raising Approaches

Traditionally, the most difficult aspect of any black campaign is fund-raising. Cooper's campaign tried a number of approaches. In the general election, two fund-raising dinners were sponsored in Prichard. The nominal cost of the tickets was still an economic hardship and attendance was poor. The only other effort initiated from the campaign office was a series of phone calls to the candidate's friends around the country and calls and visits with local potential contributors. The candidate was able to get prepaid airline tickets as a contribution to the campaign from some of these friends. The tickets were used to bring in the out-of-state political professionals.

At the national level, a "People for Cooper" fund-raising committee was formed in Washington, D.C., composed of friends and national black political leaders. A letter was sent around the country in July to friends of the candidate and members of the committee. It gave some background on the candidate, the community of Prichard and the importance of this political race. Responses to the letter were very favorable, and contributions continued to come in well into the run-off period (Exhibit #8).

Another form of campaign contribution were those items either given or loaned to the campaign by local black businessmen, individuals and organizations. These items included practically all of the office supplies and equipment used in the campaign offices.

IV. CAMPAIGN ORGANIZATION AND OPERATIONAL UNITS; GENERAL ELECTION

Staff Organization/Political Education

Before he arrived in Prichard, the campaign manager had sketched out the major units of the campaign organization to be developed, with obvious emphasis on election day activities because of the shortness of time. He had also developed a series of organizational steps. These in turn were related to the answers he would receive to a series of written background questions which would be posed at the first planning session with the candidate. Organizational decisions were then made immediately and implementation of the new campaign structure began at once. The questions related to such matters as headquarters locations, staffing and use, volunteer recruitment and use, finances, availability of demographic data, canvassing to date, media activities, the presence of scheduling and advance work, campaign literature, poll watchers, transportation, community organization, legal counsel, voter registration, local staff expertise and training, and election day activities.

The campaign manager had decided that the campaign would be organized as a total entity with every element required by the local situation, yet at the same time be related in structure to organizations normally put together for state-wide or national political campaigns. The first planning and strategy session confirmed the validity of this approach and revealed the dimensions of some of the problems which would confront political organizing in Prichard.

Because of the inexperience and lack of faith in black political know-how in the local black community, and given the late start-up time, it was felt that the campaign would have to serve as a political vehicle and also as a crash educational and motivational instrument. Every aspect of it would have to be organized in minute detail and, when time permitted, put in visual form. It had to create an instant sense of professionalism in which every activity was thoroughly planned and executed within an exact time-frame, where no function was without a system of check points, where nothing was taken for granted that could possibly be verified with exactness, where most actions would have multiple campaign purposes, and where discipline was complete.

It was immediately apparent that one of the critical ingredients upon which the success of the venture would depend would be the core of experienced political professionals from out-of-state. These professionals were from a variety of political backgrounds: the national and field staffs of presidential candidates, an assistant and campaign aide to a state legislator, an urban political strategist, a Gary, Indiana, convention organizer, political consultants, lawyers, community organizers, and media experts. Of the 13 professionals who came in, two were white.

They all had varying degrees of political expertise in local and national politics or in advanced community organization. A number of them would be the campaign coordinators of each of the operational units. Each would have a local staff counterpart assigned to work with him who had extensive community contacts or knew where the local resources were to make that unit's operation as efficient as possible. It was evident, however, that not only would the coordinators have to supervise one or more operational units, they would also have to assist in training local staff and would physically have to do much of the work themselves.

An organizational chart was developed at the first planning session, placing the coordinators and their counterparts in charge of the units where they were most effective and/or most needed. As each coordinator arrived during the hours and days that followed, he was given his assignment and briefed on political and social factors in the community, all campaign activity up to that point, all previous activity of his unit and the specific functions he was expected to perform within the deadlines established for his unit (Exhibit #9).

With the exception of the phone bank at Headquarters #2, all operational units were housed in Headquarters #1. The organizational chart, which was later reproduced, showed the units, their key personnel, and their phone extensions. The chart was distributed to all campaign staff and posted beside all campaign phones.

Simultaneous planning, organization and implementation was to continue almost around the clock until the very eve of the election as the campaign manager, the candidate, and the staff of campaign coordinators attempted to work out in hours, activities and operational units which would normally require months of preparation. They developed in meetings wedged between other activities, office procedures, lines of authority, reporting requirements, campaign strategy and organization modifications, staff orientation and training requirements, development of campaign instructions and documents, candidate events, media activity, literature distribution plans, community organizing strategies, and election day preparations and training schedules.

It was necessary for the campaign manager to conduct a number of orientation sessions with local staff on how a political campaign is organized and how it operates. The meaning and importance of the duties assigned to staff in their various units were explained, and it was stressed that the campaign would insist on an unusual degree of thoroughness in job execution and adherence to exact time schedules. The normal obligations in a campaign of doing whatever job that was assigned as opposed to doing what one wanted to do was also explained and the staff was cautioned that personal feelings about people or events associated with the campaign were not to interfere with the execution of their job. Lines of authority were outlined and staff was informed that after a full exploration of their views on an issue, the decisions of the candidate or the campaign manager were final.

The following order of discussion of the operational units in no way suggests their order of importance or a chronology of their development, since planning and implementation of everything was simultaneous.

Scheduling and Advance/Community Organization

It was critical that the candidate be placed quickly on a daily schedule to be maintained in writing by the campaign manager. This would allow the campaign to plan his activities logically in an effort to reach as many voters as possible in the time remaining, and also to prevent costly political oversights. Important groups in the community and their leaders would have to be contacted again and visited. Church schedules had to be set up for the last Sunday and major events for the last weekend would have to be planned.

Efforts were begun at once to schedule the last series of contacts and discussions with those few political figures and leaders of the larger churches, the benevolent societies, local labor and welfare rights groups. These meetings were scheduled to secure their endorsement, seek election day workers, request campaign funds and generally to encourage their more active involvement in the campaign in terms of their constituents and the larger community.

Some of the Baptist ministers within the Baptist Ministers Conference of Prichard agreed to produce and distribute sample ballots endorsing the candidate, and to permit use of churches for driver dispatch and day care on election day.

As many last-minute events for the candidate were planned as could be fitted around the campaign planning and strategy sessions. The candidate was scheduled twice during the week to visit the food stamp lines to pass out literature and stress his commitment to a food stamp mobile. Walking and shopping center tours in black neighborhoods were scheduled throughout most of the last four campaign days. The candidate was accompanied on one of the tours by Robert Hooks, formerly of T.V.'s "N.Y.P.D." program.

Churches contained the only viable public meeting facilities and this fitted well into the strategy of involving their leaders in as much campaign activity as possible. Two church rallies were planned during the latter part of the week by the Progressive Organized Workers of Prichard, a citizens' organization that had been a constant supporter of the campaign. Also, the candidate was scheduled to appear at three churches for the last Sunday and senior staff was scheduled to cover all churches to speak and pass out literature. This was followed by a motorcade through all of the heavily-populated black neighborhoods ending in a public rally at a park. The three black candidates for city council were invited to the church rallies, the motorcade and park rally with provision being made on the programs for them to present their views.

The walking tours, motorcade and park rally provided opportunities for local staff training in advance work. The campaign manager's staff briefings for these events were basically training sessions in the what and how of advancing. For the walking and shopping center tours, staff was directed to physically check out key populated areas, determine which stores or neighborhoods were to be visited, seek permission from store management on the degree of campaigning permitted, time the distance to and from the site by car, time by foot the route to be taken at the site, develop and employ handbills, media messages, leadership contacts and loud speaker systems for crowd gathering and finally, prepare a minute-by-minute schedule incorporating all of the above steps.

For the motorcade and rally, the techniques of pre-planning and checking everything associated with the event were again employed: finding a stage and getting it delivered, getting sound equipment and checking it, determining location and condition of outside electric outlets, finding entertainers and briefing them on their part in the program, arranging for security and its deployment, generating a crowd, determining the position of cars carrying local leaders in the motorcade, arranging for the decoration of cars and site, determining and pre-timing the route to be taken, seating plans for leaders at the rally site, appropriate media publicity for the event, literature distribution, insuring availability of phones at the site, concluding arrangements with park authorities, and developing the program to be presented.

As these activities were occurring, the two white staffers, in addition to their other duties, teamed with a local white volunteer for some excursions into the white community. They sought to determine if the campaign was not overreacting in its perception of negative white sentiments and to determine if some activity might appropriately be scheduled there. Their inquiries indicated that the campaign had been correct and the scheduling of an event would probably be counter-productive.

Media/Publicity

The purpose of the media section was to insure maximum media coverage of the campaign during the remaining days before the general election. The media coordinator would maintain liaison with radio, newspaper and T.V. personnel, write press releases, coordinate press conferences, make last-minute changes in media campaign ads and write speeches for major public appearances by the candidate.

The media campaign coordinator arranged a press conference, with accompanying press realeases, for Cooper and one of the white candidates for mayor to denounce the unfair voting practice of issuing ward voting lists without addresses. T.V. crews were invited to join the candidate in a visit to particularly bad examples of housing for a black and a white resident of Prichard. Coverage of the Robert Hooks visit was arranged, as well as coverage of the church rallies with the black city council candidates. For these and the park rally, major speeches were prepared by the unit.

Radio ads were also stepped up during the last four days before the election from 10 spots per day on the black stations and five per day on the white to 15 and 10 respectively. Newspaper ad copy and radio spots were written to publicize the telephone number at the phone bank and the churches which would be used as driver dispatch points for rides to the polls (Exhibit #10).

17

The endorsement of the Mobile Beacon, the black newspaper which served Prichard, was secured in time for its last Thursday edition before the election. A surprise endorsement came from the white newspaper, the Mobile Press-Register, of Cooper and a white candidate from among the field of seven running for mayor. It was the first time in the history of Mobile that the Press-Register had endorsed a black man for public office.

Volunteers

This unit was necessary to provide a central responsibility for the recruitment, assignment and coordination of volunteers. It was one of the most critical units in the campaign. Unlike such efforts in other campaigns, where volunteers supplement the regular paid staff, the volunteer coordinator would be recruiting local volunteers to man almost the entire campaign below the campaign coordinator level. Up to that point, the campaign had been relying on the services of a hard-core of about six regular volunteers at headquarters, about 10 student volunteers involved in literature distribution and nine at the phone bank.

Early planning sessions had projected an additional number of positions to be filled at the various headquarters such as drivers, more students for literature distribution, secretaries and receptionists. The projections for the operational units during election day were 147 poll watchers (three 49-man shifts), 50 canvassers (five teams of 10 each), 100 drivers for three shifts, 40 church day care supervisors (two shifts of 20 each) and 27 phone bank operators (three shifts of 9 each). When these projections were made, there was great skepticism because of poor past experience in recruiting volunteers in the city. Indeed, despite tremendous efforts, only scattered progress was made in developing the volunteer roster as election day approached. On some days the campaign had difficulty in keeping its few headquarters positions staffed for routine office functions.

The volunteer coordinator had the additional task of verifying the commitments of the four churches to be used as driver dispatch and day care centers. These churches were visited to check all information received about them: the presence of phones, the kind of child-keeping accommodations, and the number and duties of church-supplied volunteers to man the facilities. The unit coordinator also held orientation sessions for the volunteers assigned to the church centers.

Phone Bank

The phone bank was one of the means used to link the vast numbers of politically untouched black citizens of Prichard to their first real political campaign. There were nine phones and they were used to call lists of voters, leaders, women, students and professional groups to recruit volunteers. They were often kept busy calling back when volunteers failed to show up again after only one day with the campaign. The phone bank coordinator and his staff also worked continuously on finding the election day workers mentioned earlier and it was used to notify them of the time and place of their training sessions. For these functions, the phone bank coordinator trained his volunteers in the proper phone message to use and an outline of a basic conversation approach was typed and posted beside each phone.

The phone bank coordinator also used the phone bank to alert the community to the time and place of major candidate events and as a general information clearinghouse for the public on the campaign and voter registration. It also was used to conduct the poll of 400 residents.

Because citizens would only give superficial information about their families to strangers on the phone, the phone bank was not an effective instrument for phone canvassing. It was used, however, to call each black household twice and each white household once, urging them in the last few days to vote for the candidate on August 8th.

Literature Distribution/Transportation

A literature distribution unit, linked to the transportation effort, was essential to coordinate the systematic distribution of campaign literature to all neighborhoods. Because there had been little coordination or inventory control in the past, considerable waste and distribution oversights had occurred. Control was established and distribution plans with specific instructions for each type of literature were put into effect by the deputy campaign manager. Certain handbills were earmarked for the black community and others for the white, bumper stickers would thereafter be physically placed by workers on cars, not just handed out, and posters would be placed at least 13 feet above the ground so they could not be torn down easily. The campaign also offered to distribute the literature of the black candidates for city council.

Periodic orientation and training sessions were held by the deputy campaign manager with student volunteers. A rough distribution map was drawn, and by election day it showed a distribution pattern ranging from six sweeps of some black neighborhoods in the critical 2nd and 3rd wards to two sweeps in most white areas. On election eve it was arranged to have a piece of campaign literature placed in every election day morning newspaper that was delivered in the city.

It was appropriate that distribution and transportation were placed together because the distribution teams came to have first priority on available cars. Each day saw a crisis in securing enough cars or drivers to put the teams on the street and to fulfill the other normal demands of the campaign for mobility. Drivers, as with many of the other volunteers, tended to work for one day after which recruitment had to begin again. Usually local staff or the campaign coordinators would have to do whatever driving was necessary. By the weekend before election day, enough drivers had been recruited by the phone bank to begin holding election day orientation sessions. This situation was improved considerably when the campaign finally persuaded a used car dealer to donate two cars and the out-of-state coordinators, who arrived over the weekend, made their rented cars available to the campaign.

Legal Counsel

This unit was set up primarily to research Alabama election law for anything which might significantly bear on general activities on election day and specifically, on the duties and authority of poll watchers. The unit's coordinator was directed to summarize pertinent sections of the election law for inclusion as an appendix to the poll watcher's manual. He was also instructed to begin to determine if there were any legal foundation for the many rumors and assumptions that the community had carried over from the past in terms of procedures on election day. Most proved to be in error or were the result of deliberate misinformation being fed to voters.

The legal counsel unit also attempted unsuccessfully to find legal remedies for the public issuance of ward voting lists with no addresses on them. This situation posed an obviously serious problem to a black campaign in a small Southern town. For all practical purposes it voided effective voter challenges, even though such challenges are provided for in Alabama law. The fact that the voter list had not been purged of ineligible voters, that black voter registrants had been regularly discouraged and misinformed, and that black people had been excluded from any meaningful role in the official supervision of the election, had all prompted the campaign to formally request the Justice Department to send in federal observers. The unit pushed this effort and succeeded in bringing in one federal observer for election day.

Poll Watchers

History has shown the pivotal role poll watchers can play in elections in general and Southern elections in particular. In the Prichard elections of the past, when black candidates were on the ticket their poll watching had consisted of the candidate and a friend or two visiting the polling places and looking around. It was determined that the campaign's poll watcher operation would be as comprehensive as possible in this most important aspect of the election.

Campaign management attended the election officials briefing at city hall, and made verbatim notes on election day procedures and voting machine operation. The manager also attended and formally witnessed the sealing of the voting machines at the warehouse prior to their delivery to the polls in order to inspect each machine personally and record its polling place box number and identification numbers.

Training sessions for poll watchers were scheduled for the last Thursday, Saturday and Monday before the election. The black city council candidates and their staffs were invited to attend these sessions. The campaign manager had drafted the poll watcher's manual and the training sessions followed the manual's contents. The sessions that the campaign manager and his deputy conducted included information about:

1. the general responsibilities of poll watchers and their assignment and duties under Alabama law;
2. how the voting machine should be opened to prevent sabotage and what to do before the polls open;
3. what to do after the polls open and how to relate to election officials and voters;
4. the procedural requirement of watchers and officials in assisting voters;
5. how to challenge voters and report irregularities to campaign headquarters;
6. common types of election frauds;
7. what to do when the polls close and how the voting machines should be closed to prevent further voting, and

8. excerpts from Alabama election law covering these procedures.

The campaign manager began and ended each session with strong motivational messages stressing a poll watcher's right to perform his duties, the disadvantages of powerlessness and the possibility of meaningful political change in Prichard through their actions. This was done to offset a watcher's being too easily intimidated at the polls and rendered ineffective.

During the sessions, the watchers had explained to them the significance of the voting machine identification data sheet which had been prepared by the campaign to show the identification numbers of each machine, its box number (voting machine location within the poll) and its ward. A diagram of the voting machine was made which showed the location of the pertinent numbers and other important features of the machine. This was also explained. All watchers were informed that the campaign had prepared a list including every election inspector and every clerk assigned to each box in each ward and this would be given to them to help identify any officials engaged in irregularities. Finally, the campaign had designed tally sheets to be used to collect the vote totals from each machine at the end of the day. Procedures for filling out these sheets on each candidate for mayor were outlined. All of the above basic steps were also contained in the poll watcher's manual as an additional training overlay (Exhibits #11 to 15).

Voter Registration

Because of the pressures of time and the urgency of setting up so many operational units and other activities during the last ten days, voter registration activity was limited to providing information and some rides to the registrar's office through the phone bank. The campaign had decided to rest basically upon the 1,500 new voters registered by Cooper since August, 1971.

Election Day Activities

A final strategy meeting was held with the campaign coordinators the night before election to outline with charts all of the things their units had done in preparing for their responsibilities on election day. Any remaining tasks which had to be accomplished before or during election day were also charted. The deputy campaign manager was given over-all supervision of election day activites.

Phone Bank/Transportation

This unit's day began with 6:00 a.m. calls to all poll watchers, drivers, canvassers, and day care supervisors to remind them of their final briefings at headquarters that morning. The bank spent the remainder of the day calling voters urging them to go to the polls, calling the previously assembled list of those needing a ride to the polls and accepting calls from others who needed rides.

Because of these functions, transportation operations were transferred to the phone bank for election day. When drivers reported in that morning for their final instructions, a car control log was established so the campaign would know where each car was at all times. Drivers were sent to the church centers from which they were dispatched by the bank to make the pick-ups in their area. The church centers were also checked by the coordinator periodically during the day to insure they were functioning properly. The 20 drivers that did show up on election day gave the campaign a ratio of one car per 2,000 residents which was about half of the normally ideal ratio of one car per 1,000 residents, but certainly far short of the 100 cars projected for the election.

As voting patterns became more established, and based on intelligence called in from the polling places, the bank was directed to blanket those neighborhoods where there was low voter turnout with calls.

Poll Watchers

The watcher's kits were handed out by the deputy manager at their morning briefing. Each kit contained a manual, a voting machine diagram, the voting machine identification data sheet for that ward, the election official's list for that ward and the watcher's authorization certificate. The watchers were also given a one-page summary of the key points in their manuals and the tally sheet with instructions for taking the final count from each machine.

One chief poll watcher was designated for each ward and he was given that ward's voting list. A roster of the 75 watchers who reported was drawn up to show their poll assignments with whatever minimal shift changes that could be made. The chief watchers were instructed to locate primary and back-up phones at or near their polls for reporting to headquarters. The campaign coordinators, one of whom was a lawyer, were assigned to tour specific polling places all day as flying trouble shooters to back up the watchers.

This was the first time the city of Prichard had seen any candidate field the total number of poll watchers he was authorized by law to have – one poll watcher per voting machine. Their very presence and superior knowledge of election procedures intimidated most of the election officials for most of the day. As the time wore on, however, some officials became obstructive. In some places, poll watchers were not allowed to stand close enough to sign-in tables to verify from their voter list those who were voting. Instances of graveyard voting, voting by persons who were no longer residents of the city and the voting by unauthorized persons under a real voter name were reported. There were also problems with the illegal instruction of voters by some election officials inside the voting booth and some newly registered voters whose names were not on the voting lists had their voter registration certificates taken when they voted.

Legal Counsel

As all workers had been informed, the coordinator/lawyers were on call all day beside certain designated phones which were used only for reporting election irregularities. These phone numbers were also contained in the poll watcher's manuals. Contact had already been established with county legal authorities who would have to be dealt with in the event of unresolved problems and the campaign had numbers where they could be reached all day. The problems mentioned above required a number of phone conferences with county officials, and many were resolved to the campaign's satisfaction.

Vote Analysis

This unit was set up at the last minute so that running totals could be kept of the vote as this information was called into headquarters.

Canvassers

Since Alabama law prohibited the passing out of any campaign materials on election day, the canvassers stood by until dispatched by headquarters intelligence from the polling places to those neighborhoods of low voter turnout.

All campaign coordinators whose units were not specifically involved in election day activities and local staff were re-assigned to the above units and were required to report at designated intervals to headquarters. With the exception of the lawyers at the phones and the campaign manager in the command center, no other personnel were allowed in the headquarters office. During the day, no operational units failed to perform their duties. Election day was a quiet day at headquarters and there was time to plan the press conference to follow the official tallying of the vote and the receptions for the public and the staff.

Election Results

General Election Results by Ward, August 8th

Wards	1	2	3	4	5	6	AB*	Totals
V. O. Capps	272	363	183	485	344	111	4	1,762
J. Cooper	234	1,776	1,135	417	18	6	1	3,587
E. D. Jacobson	56	73	49	33	17	4		232
J. W. McNorton	27	21	18	27	46	8		147
Henry Phillips	157	149	168	139	138	39		790
Mike Saunders	10	33	7	3	3	9		65
Everette Turner	362	301	108	130	109	53		1,063
Totals	1,118	2,716	1,668	1,234	675	230	5	7,646

*Absentee Ballots.

Cooper's 3,587 votes to Capps' 1,763 in the general election was short of a majority and a run-off election was necessary.

As stated earlier, the campaign reasoned that in the general election Cooper had to show strongly over Capps in wards #2 and #3, and come as close to the incumbent as possible in wards #1 and #4, accumulating better than 4,000 votes in the process. Review of the election results indicated that, while falling short of the over-all 4,000 figure, the campaign did achieve the basic impact it sought in the four critical wards. Election data revealed that the campaign had been right in keying on wards #2 and #3. Those wards had the largest number of voters, the largest black population, and were themselves almost completely responsible for the increase in voter turnout from 6,784 in the 1968 election to the 7,646 votes cast on August 8, 1972.

For the run-off election, the campaign felt that with the anticipated voter switch-overs to the incumbent and possible voter fall-off, the candidate had to carry wards #2 and #3 at least by three to one in addition to increasing the overall vote, particularly in #1 and #4.

V. BASIC CAMPAIGN STRATEGY; RUN-OFF ELECTION

Political Premises of the Campaign

The mild shock experienced by many elements in the black and white communities at the unprecendented size of Cooper's vote in the general election changed a number of factors mentioned earlier and required some modification of campaign strategy for the run-off on September 12th. There was now general public awareness that Jay Cooper had come closer than any black man in the history of Alabama to defeating a white incumbent mayor in a general election, and regardless of the outcome of the run-off, he would remain a force to be reckoned with in the community.

It was reasoned that the political effectiveness of his campaign organization was now recognized. Many segments of both communities now believed a black man could become mayor and this suggested the need for the campaign to advance positive racial cooperation themes. Some benefit would accrue to the run-off campaign as a result of the candidate's strength in the general election, because political and community leaders who were either neutral or hostile earlier would now offer some assistance. These factors, including the record turnout, were not thought, however, to lessen the difficulties in the run-off. In spite of the strong opposition to Capps expressed in the general election, even a small voter fall-off on September 12th could assure his victory.

On the issues side, it appeared that the campaign themes had been successful, with the economic messages related to seeking outside funds, neighborhood improvement and more job opportunities striking the most receptive chords.

Black Community

The black community was astonished by the election results. The campaign reasoned that the experience had built a new sense of political awareness and confidence in the black community at large and particularly among those who had participated as volunteers. The campaign had fostered a much-needed belief in the sophistication possible in a black political organization and this would do much to offset doubts which would inevitably occur immediately after the general election about the community's ability to repeat or better its performance in the run-off. Related to this would be the difficulty of educating the still vast number of politically uninformed of the importance of voting again in a run-off election.

Particularly in wards #2 and #3 the strategy of high visibility, personal contact and citizen involvement, had succeeded in reaching the people. It was assumed that many additional leadership elements in the community would now make some overtures to the campaign. The relationship of some of them to the effort was not expected to be more than superficial, because many would still believe the campaign would fail in the run-off.

White Community

Because of media coverage of the election, a low profile in the white community was no longer necessary or indeed possible. Receptivity to the economic appeals of the campaign had been good among many elements in the white community. Since the possibility of a black mayor was now squarely before these voters, it was reasoned that a more aggressive effort for their vote could yield dividends, if tied to a sincere appeal for racial cooperation to save the city.

It was still expected, however, that a large segment of the white population would not vote for Capps and would stay home rather than vote for any black man. To assure this, the campaign again would not unduly arouse these voters by overly provocative actions.

It was also felt that a few white political and community leaders would now attempt to establish some kind of quiet relationship with the campaign.

The Incumbent

It was the campaign's premise that the election results had so shaken the incumbent that he would now have to go on the offensive at some point during the run-off and the Cooper campaign would have to respond with some vigor. The incumbent might introduce race as a divisive issue and probably would begin a quiet intimidation effort in the poor black neighborhoods. While the incumbent and his forces had been totally unprepared for the efficiency of Cooper's organization and thoroughness of its trained workers, particularly on election day, he would not be caught off guard again. Finally, his silence on the out-of-state political organizers in Cooper's campaign was uncharacteristic for the South.

General Campaign Themes and Approaches

These new judgements necessitated new strategic approaches. The possibility in the public mind of a black mayor of Prichard, coupled with the decision to move aggressively for the white vote, required a modification of campaign themes to counter the anticipated introduction of racism by the incumbent, and to extend the hand of cooperation publicly to white voters. The citizens, black and white, would now be urged to work with Cooper and "together" they could save Prichard from bankruptcy and improve the quality of all their lives. It would be stressed again that the candidate would help them improve their neighborhoods, and bring efficiency and honesty to government. His ability to attract federal and private resources from outside of Prichard would again be emphasized.

These themes would be expressed in a new series of campaign literature and media messages. They would also become the basis as before of all public statements and provide the motive for events and activities by the candidate. In addition, it became strategically meaningful now to bring in respected national dignitaries to dramatize and epitomize certain campaign themes. These activities would be woven into a continuous series of events and press releases to command an even greater share of media space and time to make the candidate and the campaign as highly visible as possible.

Black Community

Efforts would have to be made in the black community to hold the approximately 3,400 black votes received in the general election and to motivate a good portion of the 4,100 black registrants who did not vote. Added to these efforts would be a new major voter registration drive to gain as much insurance as possible against any degree of voter fall-off. There would be multiple phone canvassing of the black community urging registration and voting.

Attempts would be made to recruit additional volunteers from every age and income level for literature distribution. The personal contact of these campaign workers with the voters would be increased through a minutely detailed city-wide distribution schedule. The religious community would be tied into all public events on behalf of the candidate and visiting dignitaries. The organization of a massive effort to gain small campaign contributions as a method of securing personal attachments to the campaign would be implemented. New efforts would be made to involve additional leadership elements and professional and social organizations as volunteers.

Media advertising would be intensified and public exposure of the candidate would be increased along with visual association with, and endorsement by, key national personalities in the black political and civil rights world.

White Community

The new campaign literature contained a handbill specifically addressed to the white community. This item along with the other new themes, with their stress on racial cooperation and economic improvement, would become the basis for a new, more intense white media publicity effort. The literature would also be scheduled this time for saturation distribution in the white community. Contact would be made with a number of political and community leaders to enlist their aid in gaining entry into white civic clubs, businesses and homes for informal get-acquainted sessions. The feasibility of the candidate campaigning at George Wallace's Labor Day rally would be discussed.

The Incumbent

The new literature was also developed with the incumbent in mind. The appeal for racial harmony to save the city was combined with a slightly harder stand on the economic and social issues in an effort to preempt both of those areas from whatever negative offensive Capps might mount later. It was planned, if the incumbent attacked the campaign, to counter with already researched and prepared statements on his subversion of the criminal courts, his deception of the citizens about the inflow of resources to the community and on corruption in city hall. These statements would relate these practices to the general economic decline of the city and the waste of citizen tax dollars.

Campaign Publicity

As indicated earlier, modification and tightening of the campaign themes became necessary. Four new pieces of literature were developed by the candidate and the campaign manager for distribution, and they focused on Cooper as the candidate who would work with black and white people to save the city. The people were reminded in stronger terms than during the general election of the corruption and inefficiency which had wasted their tax dollars and brought the city to the point of near-bankruptcy. The citizens were cautioned against attempts to divide them along racial lines, to obscure their recognition and resolution of their problems. Cooper's ability to put the city's finances in order and bring in the necessary outside resources to create an expanded job market were repeated. "Save Prichard" became "Together we can save Prichard " (Exhibits #16 to 19).

Although one of the new pieces was specifically geared to a white audience, all of the other pieces could be used interchangeably in either community. Ten thousand of each were produced locally, as well as additional bumper and lapel stickers, and large posters. Their messages were again the basis for new newspaper ads and radio spots, adding a voter registration plea to tie them into the new registration drive.

Radio spot scripts were also developed by the campaign manager for key black entertainers combining themes from their hit records with campaign themes and with appeals to register and vote for the candidate. The same approach was used for a ranking U.S. Senator (Exhibits #20-21).

Fund Raising Approaches

In the run-off campaign, a fund-raising letter was drafted by local staff to be used in the Prichard/Mobile area. It was signed by the co-chairwomen of the Women for Cooper organization. In addition to the contacts of these widely respected community leaders, the letter was sent to a list of persons who regularly contributed to civic causes in Mobile County. The letter stressed the political record set in the general election, outlined some of Prichard's problems and requested a contribution (Exhibit #22).

Individual letters were also drafted this time and mailed to wealthy friends and associates of the candidate, and most produced good results (Exhibit #23). There were still the calls and visits with potential local contributors. Other sources of funds were a cabaret planned with black candidates for city council, a fashion show and beauty contest planned by the Women for Cooper organization and collections from the rallies and events held in the churches.

One of the more ambitious fund-raising ventures undertaken during the run-off was a massive, city-wide, nickel and dime campaign. During the general election, student volunteers had often used crude containers with campaign materials attached to them to collect money to feed those who worked all day distributing campaign literature. During the run-off a test was conducted to determine how effective such a campaign might be if conducted on a large scale. Eight student volunteers were sent to intersections, shopping centers and liquor stores. In three hours, they had collected over $200.

It was decided to cover the city with such an effort on the last weekend of the run-off campaign. Not only would a substantial sum be collected, but it would be an ideal mechanism for last-minute involvement of the 18 year old voters. It would also present an opportunity for personal contact between a large number of voters and campaign workers at every major intersection, shopping center and heavily populated neighborhood in town on the critical last weekend. The act of giving, if nothing more than a dime, would still give people an attachment to the campaign that might pay dividends on September 12th (Exhibits #24 to 26).

Black businessmen, individuals and organizational contributions of goods, services, supplies and equipment to the campaign increased during the run-off election. When the main staff moved to headquarters #3, that office was fully equipped by such contributions. Such contributions also included making minor repairs around the offices. Other black businessmen who owned night clubs were just as generous in allowing the campaign to use their facilities, free of charge, to hold various events.

VI. CAMPAIGN ORGANIZATION AND OPERATIONAL UNITS; RUN-OFF ELECTION

Staff Organization/Political Education

The organizational structure that the campaign used in the general election had proved its effectiveness and the same structure would now be carried over into the run-off. A number of factors, however, would now require that the structure be used in a slightly different way. Changes in the mood of the community after the general election had prompted changes in strategy and operational procedure. Lessons learned about how each unit operated best would have to be incorporated into its future functions, increased staff skills would have to be properly utilized through upgrading in responsibility and reassignment, and projected new activities would have to be folded into the appropriate units.

Local staff had advanced considerably in their knowledge of campaigning. During the period immediately after the general election, local staff had taken up early planning of the voter registration drive, the local fund raising project, resumed phone bank operations and had started to distribute literature left over from the general election. These plans were expanded upon in early staff meetings with the campaign manager. Because there was now more time, the daily local staff meetings afforded another occasion for staff training in the mechanics of planning and carrying out projects in a political campaign and the importance of working within established time frames. The sessions were also used to continue to reinforce such basic campaign procedures as clearing appointments, assignments, program schedules and community leader contacts with the campaign manager or candidate before such actions were taken. The importance of working with all kinds of people for an overriding political objective even if one had deep personal or ideological differences with some of them was stressed again. Minutes of the meetings were typed and distributed to all local staff members as an instructional tool.

All three headquarters were fully activated now. Headquarters #1 would continue to be used for the literature distribution unit and Legal Counsel. The nickel and dime effort was added. Headquarters #2 would continue to house the phone bank. Because of the working relationship between the two, the voter registration unit was also placed there. Headquarters #3 became the main campaign headquarters and would have the scheduling and advance, transportation, press and poll watchers and a special community organization unit. An organizational chart was again prepared reflecting the location and staff changes, and distributed and posted as in the general election.

By the time the out-of-state coordinators began to arrive in late August, local staff members were able to supervise effectively the phone bank and literature distribution operations and a number of activities within the other units. As the coordinators reported in, each was again matched with his counterpart who now assumed a substantial part of the supervision of the unit. The coordinators were given their in-depth briefings on the changes in the local political situation; the modified organizational structure and their assignments, past activities of the units, and new projects to be undertaken and their time tables (Exhibit #27).

Scheduling and Advance/Community Organization

With more time available, daily written schedules were now prepared and given to the candidate (Exhibit #28). All campaign events and other activities were also charted daily on large handmade wall calendars. In keeping with the strategy of even greater visibility during the run-off, more critical leadership meetings, organizational contacts, and media events were scheduled.

As anticipated, the general election results had motivated additional black leadership to become involved in the campaign. The suggestion of a Women for Cooper organization was quickly picked up by local black women leaders and over 150 women, a record for Prichard, turned out for a series of scheduled meetings with the candidate and the campaign manager to discuss ways in which they could help. By mid-August, the ladies had broken down the black neighborhoods in the city into nine districts, each of which would have a team captain and a core of workers to canvass door-to-door on the voter registration drive.

A number of major activities grew out of these scheduled meetings. The campaign tied the ladies' organizational structure into its literature distribution plan and the nickel and dime campaign using their core of workers and the same district units. A speaking outline was prepared for representatives of the ladies' organization, covering the voter registration effort, absentee ballots, campaign volunteers and getting-out-the-vote (Exhibit #29). The outline was used by their representatives in every black church in Prichard. A meeting was scheduled for the ladies with the black candidates for city council so the candidates, along with

Cooper as principal speaker, could present their views and discuss the involvement of the ladies' organization in the campaigns of all of the black candidates (Exhibit #30). The ladies' organization became one of the most vital elements of the campaign in the community.

Representatives of all of the black social clubs in the Mobile County area were invited to a meeting with the candidate to discuss their support of the campaign and volunteer needs.

Meetings between the candidate, the older political figures and religious leaders were rescheduled and general commitments of support were received. Cooper scheduled meetings with student leaders at the two largest high schools in the city to ask for their support in helping to get volunteers for the literature and nickel and dime efforts. The black candidates for city council were invited by Cooper to a series of meetings to discuss additional cooperative efforts and to stress the danger to them of their low visibility.

The candidate scheduled appointments with white opponents defeated during the general election campaign and with other white political and community leaders to discuss the possibility of addressing such groups as the local Kiwanis, Civitan and Rotary Clubs and to explore again informal meetings in white homes. The two most critical groups of white city employees in Prichard, the police and firemen, were visited by the candidate at their stations to discuss local issues and job tenure. Most of Labor Day was scheduled for the candidate to campaign among the crowd at the George Wallace rally, where responses were much more favorable than expected.

As indicated earlier, a number of dignitaries were invited in to dramatize the campaign themes of urban governmental reform, interracial cooperation and to exemplify the campaign promise that Cooper could bring to Prichard important human and financial resources.

The first political dignitary to come to the city to campaign on behalf of Cooper was Atlanta's Vice Mayor Maynard Jackson. His visit was used by the campaign manager as an educational vehicle for staff on the preparation, treatment and scheduling of important national figures. News releases were prepared in advance of his arrival and used by all media. An airport press conference was arranged, and a reception committee of prominent citizens was set up to greet the vice mayor on his arrival. A minute-by-minute schedule was advanced and prepared for distribution to the media, the dignitary, staff and local leaders (Exhibit #31). Programs were prepared for all the events the vice mayor would participate in and they also were appropriately distributed.

Although later working within a tighter time-frame, this approach was the model for the following visits of Mayor Richard Hatcher and Rev. Ralph David Abernathy. It was also a very conscious method of showing the entire community how national black leadership should be properly honored through well-planned and well-executed events, and it reflected the gratitude of the campaign that these leaders took time from their schedules to help a black community achieve political power. This approach caused Mayor Hatcher's and Rev. Abernathy's joint election eve rally to be the best-attended and most enthusiastic political event in the memory of the city (Exhibit #32).

A number of walking and shopping center tours were arranged again and a fashion show and cabaret were scheduled. There were additional church rallies, including three gospel programs. On the final weekend, the largest motorcade Prichard had ever seen was organized for the candidate, ending in a giant parade. Just as in the general election, the black candidates for city council were invited to attend all of the major functions planned for Cooper in the run-off and provisions were made for them to present their platform to the people.

Media/Publicity

The candidate arranged a series of meetings to develop the new campaign newspaper ads and radio spots and contacts were made with national black and white media outlets to inform them of campaign progress (Exhibit #33). The scheduling of events and dignitary arrivals was such that media coverage expanded significantly during the last half of August. There was almost continuous daily coverage of the campaign and the candidate during the last 10 days before the election (Exhibit #34).

As anticipated, the incumbent broke his silence after Maynard Jackson's visit, but made the tactical error of attacking the campaign where it was strongest, and he the weakest. He denounced the "outside influences and money" being brought to bear in Cooper's campaign and followed this with ads outlining all the federal programs he purportedly had brought into Prichard. This was the first public sign that Capps was being hurt by one of the main strategic approaches of the campaign. The candidate replied with the obvious thrust that, just as he had been saying, the visits proved his intention to bring in needed outside resources for whatever purposes in direct opposition to the incumbent's record in this area.

The candidate followed this with a series of news conferences exposing the inaccuracy of Capps' claims of bringing in federal programs, again knowing the incumbent's own record made such stands by him obviously political and unsupportable. Other press conferences, newspaper ads and radio spots against Capps during the last week of the campaign discussed the incumbent's failure to disclose his real income or to explain the expensive hidden yacht he kept, documented evidence of unauthorized waiving of thousands of dollars in court fines, his failure to get a fair share of state funds for Prichard, his ridiculous attempt to claim credit for bringing in federal observers for the run-off election, and his responsibility for the smear sheets and race-baiting literature then appearing on city streets (Exhibits #35-36).

The Mobile Press - Register endorsed Jay Cooper over the incumbent in the run-off, but did not endorse any of the black candidates for city council. This generated much campaign discussion of the possible divisive overtones of such an action in the black community and steps were immediately taken to offset it through a series of meetings with the other black candidates, and renewed pledges of solidarity and mutual support among black candidates at all public functions.

New radio spots were written, giving phone numbers for a ride to the polls and asking for student volunteers for literature distribution (Exhibits #37-38).

Volunteers

As indicated earlier, although many more people were now involved in campaign projects in the community, the number willing to volunteer for essential headquarters work did not materially increase (Exhibit #39). On some days, literature distribution, phone bank, voter registration and the transportation systems were seriously hampered because of lack of volunteers and the burden of accomplishing that day's activities would fall completely on the small core of local staff. This situation improved somewhat in late August, but was made tenuous again in September when school went back in session a week before the run-off. This involved the students and most of the professionals in back-to-school preoccupations.

The volunteer recruitment assignments for the run-off were

considerably more moderate than during the general election. The volunteer coordinator had the names of those who had worked with the campaign during the general election, and they were called to remind them of upcoming orientation meetings. It was now estimated that the campaign might probably get only the 49 poll watchers it absolutely had to have, nine volunteers for all-day phone bank operations, and very few canvassers. Efforts would still be made to get 100 drivers.

The volunteer coordinator again verified the use of churches as driver dispatch centers. There was no need during the run-off to provide more than one day care facility because the campaign had found during the general election that mothers were reluctant to leave their children with strangers while going to vote.

Phone Bank

The primary mission of the phone bank in early and mid-August was to organize its various lists of citizens in definite categories such as religious leaders, general community leaders, unregistered black voters, black and white registered voters, women, social organizations, students, and professional groups. After the voter registration drive started on August 19th, the phone bank became the principal contact mechanism for reaching the unregistered black voters and coordinating their transportation. The bank continued up to election day its calls to recruit volunteers and notify them of meetings and to alert the community to major planned events. It also continued as the general information clearinghouse for the campaign until this function later became so hectic that a staff person was designated at the main headquarters to handle all such calls.

Toward the end of August, as the phone bank coordinator began to prepare to blanket the city three times just before the election, a new phone conversation format for the operators was developed by the campaign manager. It emphasized the importance of voting again in the run-off, gave the phone number for a ride to the polls and requested volunteers. Volunteer information was placed on a newly-developed volunteer utilization form (Exhibits #40–41)

Literature Distribution/Transportation

The campaign was proud of its new literature and the candidate wished to have the most effective distribution plan possible. The campaign manager instructed staff to develop two maps, one showing population concentrations by a color key and overlaying on it the women's nine registration districts, plus the all-white neighborhood. The other map would show the ward boundary lines (See maps #1 & 2). He instructed the distribution coordinator to develop a written plan to show which piece of literature or bumper sticker, lapel sticker and poster in what quantity would be in what shopping center, intersection, church, business center and neighborhood within which district on each day from September 4th to election eve. The literature would be coded alphabetically and distribution would be planned so that general-appeal pieces would hit every city neighborhood at least once; the white-oriented pieces to those neighborhoods at least twice. The other pieces were targeted to key neighborhoods in the 1st, 2nd, 3rd and 4th wards at least four times, and all pieces would be used up by the night before the election (Exhibit #42).

When this plan was completed, the campaign manager plotted its distribution pattern on a chart to show the number of times a piece hit a district, the spread of various pieces among the districts, and the interval of distribution. Adjustments were then made in the distribution plan to eliminate imbalances which appeared on this chart. In addition to this, campaign coordinators and the candidate stayed up all night on a number of occasions, putting up posters when this part of the plan fell behind schedule for lack of volunteers.

A special letter was drafted and mailed to all registered white voters over the last weekend of the campaign stressing economic themes and asking their support. The campaign also distributed sample ballots over the entire city the night before the election in order to prevent alteration (Exhibits #43–44).

As in the general election, transportation problems plagued the run-off. The campaign could not afford to hire drivers and it was never able to get a stable core of volunteers for this purpose. This caused daily problems in literature distribution and voter registration. The campaign was able to get two used cars donated again, and they were used as general headquarters transportation and fall-back vehicles for the above tasks. Anticipating heavy last-minute registration on the Monday before election and a short supply of cars on election day, the candidate was able to get a special contribution which allowed the campaign to rent ten cars for those two days.

Legal Counsel

One of the first jobs the legal coordinator/lawyer was directed to do was to research the requirements for absentee voting. This was important because many black students who had voted for the candidate in the general election would now be away at college on run-off election day. The other urgent task was to recheck Alabama election law to see if there were any remedies for some of the more serious problems encountered at the polls on August 8th.

It was determined that there was no specifications in law on where poll watchers could stand, or on the need to provide ward voting lists with addresses. There were, however, prohibitions against writing materials inside polling places and against election officials going behind the curtain in the voting booth to assist voters, as they had done in the general election. Because of the strategic importance of newly-registered voters to the campaign, the unit was also to determine how these voters, whose names were not on the voting list in the general election, could now vote in the run-off since their registration certificates had been attached to the challenge paper ballots that they were required to vote. It was found that the surrender of the certificates was not a legal requirement. Further action on this was averted when Mobile County officials announced the issuance of a supplemental voting list to include all new registrants up to August 19th. Those registering beyond that date in the new registration drive would, of course, have their registration certificates when they went to the polls. They would again, under the Alabama law, be required to vote a challenge paper ballot in the run-off.*

During this same time, the remaining problems which prevented effective challenge of unauthorized voters were documented and a second request was made to the Justice Department for federal observers, two weeks before Capp's alleged request for their assistance. Two observers arrived the week before the election to investigate these irregularities and two more were on hand on election day.

The Legal Counsel determined that adjustments in the language of the poll watcher's manual for the run-off election were so minor that they could be thoroughly covered in training sessions, and the same manual would be used again.

Poll Watchers

Preparations for this unit began with a poll watcher's feedback meeting with the campaign manager in mid-August to discuss

---

*Under Alabama law, a newly-registered voter whose name is not yet on the voting list at the polls is required to vote a paper challenge ballot instead of voting on the voting machine.

problems encountered during the last election and to tell the poll watchers the steps the campaign was taking to resolve them. The feedback meeting was also used to relate their anger and frustrations with their treatment by election officials to their political powerlessness, and to point up the need because of this for redoubling their advocacy of the campaign among friends in the community.

The campaign manager and the deputy again made a point of attending the election inspector's briefing at city hall. Mayor Capps was on hand this time to guide discussion and it became apparent that because of the wide latitude Alabama election law gives local election officials, the poll watchers this time would be even more severely restricted in activity and movement within the polling place. The election inspectors, as the officials in charge of the polls, were told they could decide all matters not expressly covered by law, and their decisions could not be challenged by any authority on election day. The net effect of this would be that the campaign's poll watchers would not be able to observe voter sign-in or take periodic counts of the vote. Their effectiveness, for all practical purposes, would be reduced to reporting gross irregularities and showing by their very presence the continued persistence and determination of the campaign. It was clear the incumbent would have to be beaten by the sheer weight of votes, since there would be no way to prevent countless illegal votes under the present constraints.

Other activities in preparation for the poll watchers training sessions included witnessing again the sealing of the voting machines and identifying them by number, ward and box location. The order of placement of the candidates' names on the voting machine ballot was also of special interest because an exact diagram of the voting machine ballot had been prepared for a voter education program for the new voters. It was being held up until visual confirmation of exact name placement had been made by the campaign manager, even though the city clerk had supplied the information by phone earlier.

Later, the three poll watcher training sessions were conducted in the same detail as before, on the last Thursday, Saturday and Monday before the election. At those times, the answers supplied by legal research to some of the earlier problems were conveyed to poll watchers, including such details as the five minute maximum time a voter could be in the voting booth. This data was also presented to the black city council candidates. The manual and

40

the other documents in the watcher's kits remained the same but new voting machine identification data sheets and vote tally sheets had to be prepared (Exhibit #45).

Voter Registration

A new voter registration drive directed by local staff was ordered as insurance against any voter fall-off and to compensate for the votes that would be lost due to irregularities the campaign knew it would not be able to detect. The plan for the registration drive was quite simple and related to the Prichard situation. The Women for Cooper organization would canvass every black household in town handing out an instruction sheet on how to register which had been prepared by the manager. They also noted on a canvass form appropriate registration information about that household for the phone bank (Exhibits #46,-47). At the same time, the phone bank, using the canvass forms and the list it already had of unregistered black voters, called the residence and arranged a time for these voters to be picked up by car, taken to the registrar's office, and returned. The goal was 1,000 new black voters between the day the registrar's office opened on August 19th and September 12th, the day of the run-off.

It was estimated that taking into consideration Sundays and a half day on Saturdays, if at least 50 people could be registered each day, the campaign would have 1,050 new voters by September 12th. On the Saturday the registrar's office opened the campaign registered 300 new voters by noon. Thereafter, regular reports of the count, which averaged about 40 per day, were given at daily staff meetings and the strategies discussed for improving the effort were incorporated into minutes of the meeting as staff reminders (Exhibit #48). An absentee ballot information sheet was also prepared based on the legal research and a limited number of copies given to all of the women district captains, staff and posted by all campaign phones. The detailed diagram of the voting machine ballot was reproduced after it had been verified and also given to the district captains. This instruction sheet showed the new voter where Cooper's name would be on the voting machine, told him how to operate the machine and cast a vote for the candidate. The diagram was also used in voter education classes the morning of the run-off election. These were held in churches by the Women for Cooper organization. The times and locations for these classes were announced over the radio (Exhibits #49 to 51).

Black radio stations were persuaded to urge voter registration with public service announcements. Paid campaign radio spots gave the number of the phone bank to call for a ride to be registered and two radio programs were arranged so campaign staff could describe how to register. Churches and social organizations were asked to notify their members of the effort.

On the first day of registration, county officials at the registrar's office engaged in obvious delaying and harassment tactics. This infuriated community leaders assigned by the campaign to the registrar's office to assist the new registrants. Again, these experiences were used by the manager in all subsequent community and staff meetings to attack voter apathy by illustrating from the experiences of the people the penalties of political powerlessness.

As election day approached, the registration drive increased and ten cars were rented for the Monday before election to handle the appointments being set up by the phone bank for rides to register and the increasing number of call-ins by persons wanting rides.

Election Day Activities

Although routines were pretty much set in everyone's mind by then, a check list was nevertheless prepared to review election day procedures at the last staff meeting the night before the election. The deputy campaign manager was again placed in charge of election day events.

Driver dispatch was transferred completely to the phone bank and over 40 cars were available for duty. The precision with which they were dispatched by local staff personnel added substantially to the candidate's margin of victory. The flying poll watcher trouble shooters carried out their normal duties and other election day activities remained basically the same. The problems at the polls came mostly when election officials sought to prevent or delay the new registrants from voting. As the campaign identified such problems, trouble shooters or a federal observer were dispatched to the scene.

As before, the headquarters command center was quiet and there were no organizational mishaps. As a final imaginative campaign touch, when the candidate on his poll inspection tour noticed extremely long lines of voters waiting in the very hot sun of Prichard to vote at city hall, he secured tents within minutes and arranged to have them set up for the voters to stand under. Staff members arranged cool drinks for them and offered to hold their place in line if they wished to sit down.

Election Results

The following are the election results:

RUN-OFF ELECTION RESULTS BY WARD, SEPTEMBER 12, 1972

Ward	1	2	3	4	5	6	AB	Totals
V. O. Capps.....	889	1,051	664	1,116	968	342	21	5,057
C.B............	68	64	79	92	68	51		
A. Jay Cooper	384	2,723	1,749	638	68	30	8	5,601
C.B............	59	516	401	110	8	5		
Totals...............	1,273	3,774	2,413	1,754	1,036	372	29	10,658
C.B............	127	580	480	202	76	56		

CB - Challenge Ballots*
AB - Absentee Ballots

Although the results reveal large voter swings to the incumbent in wards #1, 4, 5 and 6, Cooper still held his ground fairly well in wards #1 and 4. The candidate won the election by carrying wards #2 and 3 by almost three to one and most importantly, by the extra margin given him by the newly registered black voters. Of 1,521 challenge ballots cast, over two-thirds, or 1,103, were cast for the new mayor of Prichard, Alabama.

Applicability of Campaign Techniques to Other Locations

The purpose of this study is to show how an advanced campaign organization with all of the essential operational units necessary for the community, was brought to a southern town. It shows why each unit was needed and some general overview of what each unit did. The study also seeks to explain how a campaign organization can be developed and used in a black community to carry out necessary political tasks and at the same time politically educate a constituency.

While describing what was done in the campaign, the study cannot relate the normal political intangibles of a campaign. It cannot describe the sense of knowing how to use the potential of each operational unit, of knowing which of the many kinds of things

---

*For the purposes of this study, the challenge ballots (CB) which the newly registered voters were required to vote were isolated in a separate column under each ward, although they are in fact incorporated in the ward votes shown.

possible for a given unit would actually be done with that unit in that community, how they would be done, when and to whom. Such intangibles usually will determine that organizational structures be used in very different ways in different communities.

A typical example of this was the organizational structure decided on for Prichard. That structure took into consideration the shortness of time in both campaigns, the size of the community and the campaign and the local level of political awareness and experience. As indicated earlier, the structure was composed of eight operational units. In another campaign four of those units, literature distribution/transportation, phone bank, poll watchers and voter registration would probably have been designated only as campaign activities within a larger operational unit. It was necessary in Prichard that they become operational units themselves.

The study also does not discuss the various expansions of campaign structure which might be necessary for other communities such as 1) various kinds of committees; citizens, youth, women, finance, political/advisory; 2) additional operational units; field operations, finance, administration, etc.; 3) numerous campaign activities, such as speaker's bureau, polling, research, boiler room, fund raising, poll workers, direct mail, issues task force, travel and budget, or 4) the many possible subdivisions of any given unit such as the normal sections one might find under a communication unit; a news release section, radio-press-TV, special interest press, photo file section, issues and speech section, clipping and transcript section, press kits and information, public information, and so forth.

One of the reasons why some black candidates experience difficulties in their bid for elective office is that campaign organizations are put together which do not have many of the vital operational units needed for that community or the units that are functioning are not fully exploited. Unless one is a black incumbent, with a well-developed and highly disciplined political organization, it may be a waste of resources to set up anything but a complete campaign structure. Even with such a structure and staff and given a voter population that makes success a good probability, the organizational structure itself still is not a guarantee of victory. It should be noted that despite many of the things done with the structure in Prichard, that election was still extremely close. On the other hand, the absence of any one of those operational units could have cost the election.

The campaign structure described in this study, with modifications for large urban areas, would be useful for campaigns ranging from that of county commissioner to U.S. Congressman. The strategies and approach, however, would have to be tailored to the particular community, but that rule of politics which demands strict attention to time and detail would be the same. Such an approach would yield substantial dividends in countless counties, cities and state legislative districts in the South where black population percentages could do much to assure victory. It will be most useful to view this approach in relation to those 59 congressional districts around the country which have a 30 percent or more black population. Significantly, 33 of these districts are in the South.* It can also be used by black candidates in communities which have very small black populations, in which the candidates must develop a campaign based on coalitions with white groups.

As the national black community becomes more and more aware of the importance of political power as a prerequisite to improving the quality of black lives, it is important that some mechanism be developed to assemble and make available skilled black political technicians. Such a mechanism is necessary so that when black candidates run for elective office, they do not have to continuously re-invent the wheel, that is, learn the basics of political organization as if such knowledge did not already exist. Such a mechanism would be useful until political skills have been sufficiently distributed in the national black community to offset the generations of exclusion from the political process, and it is realized that the majority community does not hold exclusive rights to political expertise.

* * *

FINAL NOTE:

With campaign workers on hand behind each voting machine as it was opened at the end of the day on September 12th to record the vote tally, and then waiting out the counting of the challenge ballots, the campaign knew before anyone else that its main campaign slogan, "Save Prichard" had come true.

And so, on the inscription on a silver key chain later given to campaign staff, another small victory was declared — "Prichard Saved."

---

*JCPS Research Bulletin, Vol. 1, No. 3, Mar., 1972, "The Black Electorate: A Statistical Summary."

Appendix

The following exhibits are only a small number of the many documents used in the campaign. Some are examples of many similar documents prepared by the campaign, such as news paper ads, radio spots, press releases, schedules, etc. Others are one of a kind documents prepared for specific purposes such as the handbills, poll watcher's manual, staff and community instructions and education materials.

General Election

Run-Off Election

Plate No. 1

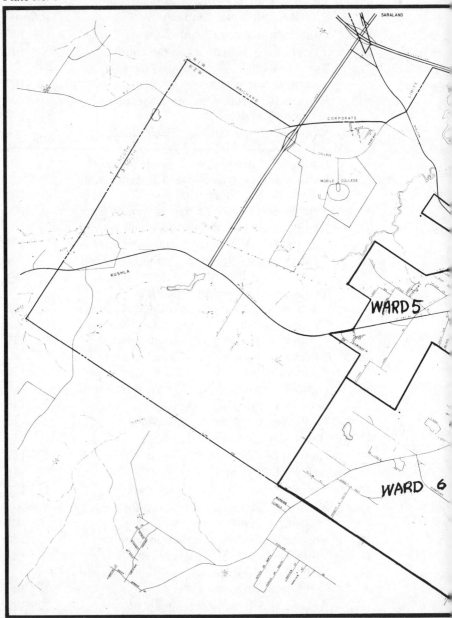

Map showing black population concentrations in Prichard

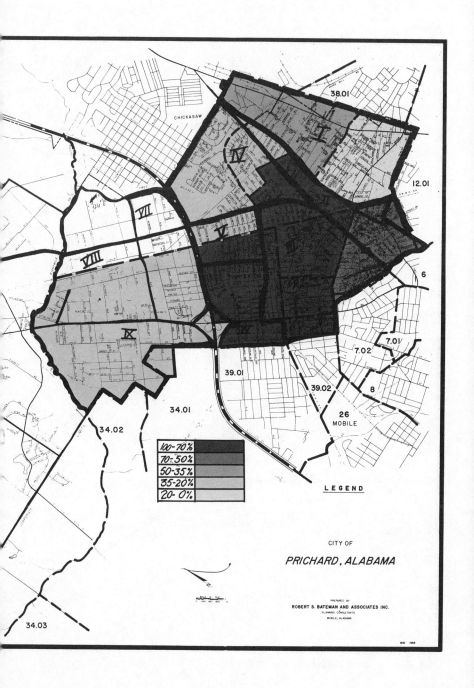

CHICKASAW

38.01

12.01

6

7.01

7.02

39.01

39.02

8

26
MOBILE

34.01

34.02

34.03

100-70%	
70-50%	
50-35%	
35-20%	
20-0%	

LEGEND

CITY OF

PRICHARD, ALABAMA

PREPARED BY

ROBERT S. BATEMAN AND ASSOCIATES INC.
PLANNING CONSULTANTS
MOBILE, ALABAMA

MAY 1968

Plate No. 2

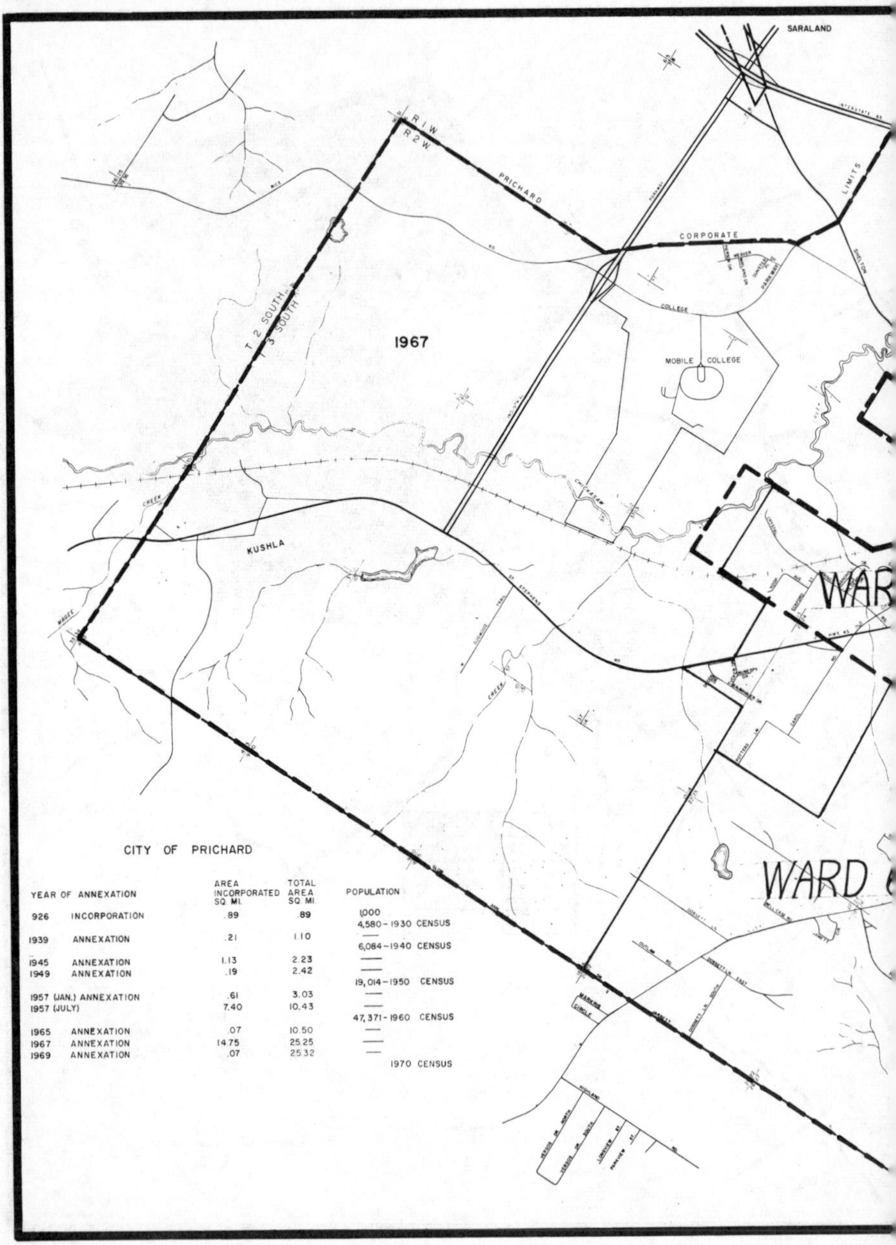
SARALAND
R 1 W
R 2 W
PRICHARD
CORPORATE
LIMITS
1967
T 2 SOUTH
T 3 SOUTH
COLLEGE
MOBILE COLLEGE
CHICKASAW
CREEK
KUSHLA
ST. STEPHENS
MAGEE
WAR
HWY 45
WARD
CITY OF PRICHARD
YEAR OF ANNEXATION
AREA INCORPORATED SQ. MI.
TOTAL AREA SQ. MI.
POPULATION
926 INCORPORATION .89 .89
1,000
4,580 – 1930 CENSUS
1939 ANNEXATION .21 1.10
6,084 – 1940 CENSUS
1945 ANNEXATION 1.13 2.23
1949 ANNEXATION .19 2.42
19,014 – 1950 CENSUS
1957 (JAN.) ANNEXATION .61 3.03
1957 (JULY) 7.40 10.43
47,371 – 1960 CENSUS
1965 ANNEXATION .07 10.50
1967 ANNEXATION 14.75 25.25
1969 ANNEXATION .07 25.32
1970 CENSUS

Map showing ward boundary lines in Prichard

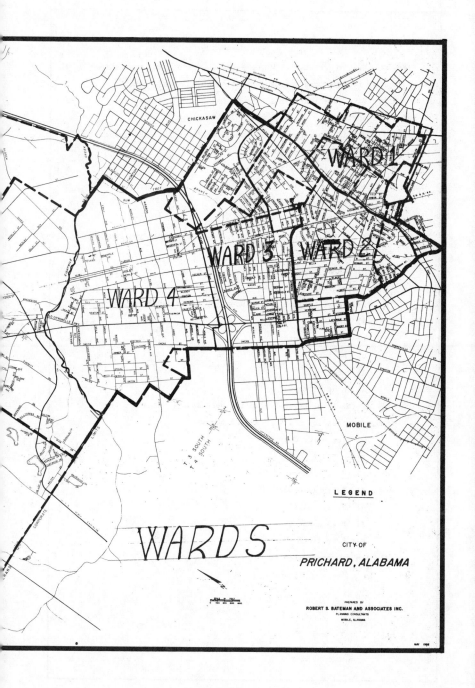

CHICKASAW

WARD 1

WARD 3   WARD 2

WARD 4

MOBILE

LEGEND

WARDS

CITY OF
PRICHARD, ALABAMA

PREPARED BY
ROBERT S. BATEMAN AND ASSOCIATES INC.
PLANNING CONSULTANTS
MOBILE, ALABAMA

MAY 1966

Hello, Mr. or Mrs....... My name is...... and I am conducting
a survey for American Independent Research. I would like to
ask you five questions pertaining to matters of national and
local importance.

1) What do you regard as the most important national issue.

    a) The Vietnam War

    a) The state of the economy

    c) Law and order

    d) Honesty in government

    e) Taxes

2) If the Presidential election were today, would you support:

    a) President Nixon

    b) Senator McGovern

    c) neither or someone else

3) What do you regard as the most important local issue:

    a) Taxes

    b) Unemployment

    c) Busing

    d) Ecology

    e) none of these

4) If the local mayoral election were today, who would be
your first choice and your second choice:

    a) Vernon O. Capps

    b) A "Jay" Cooper

c)   c) E. D. Jacobson

    d) Jerry MoNorton

    e) Henry Phillips

    f) Mike Sanders

    g) Everette L. Turner

5) Are you registered to vote?

Questionnaire prepared for poll of voters

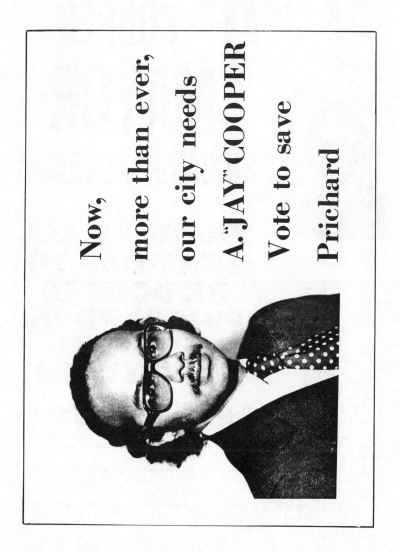

Handbill using campaign themes

ELECT
A. "JAY" COOPER
MAYOR
PRICHARD, ALABAMA

THINK OF ALL THAT HAS TO BE DONE IN PRICHARD IN THE NEXT FOUR YEARS

A Program For Progress To Save Prichard

Prichard is a city with a great potential to be prosperous economically, clean environmentally, and to have an honest city government which is not in debt.

Prichard can have full employment and programs to train employees. Prichard can be a place with good housing, good streets and good drainage and also Prichard can reduce pollution.

Prichard can be a city which cares - cares for its residents and cares for its employees; cares for its old people and cares for its poor people; cares for its young people and for its veterans who have fought to protect us.

Prichard can be a city of peace, where people live together in harmony without riots and boycotts and with respect, decency and proper treatment of all people.

I believe I am the only candidate who can save Prichard for all of us.

Handbill using campaign themes

SAMPLE BALLOT

VOTE
for
Honesty,
New Jobs,
New Industry,
Clean Streets

FOR YOUR CONVENIENCE

MAYOR
( ) Vernon O. Capps
( ) A. "Jay" Cooper, Jr.
( ) E. D. Jacobson
( ) Jerry W. McNorton
( ) Henry W. Phillips
( ) Mike Sanders
( ) Everette L. Turner

PLACE 1
( ) Homer Glenn Cagle
( ) Handy L. Davis
( ) Edward "Joe" Graham
( ) Johnny Pogue
( ) W. M. Shaw, Jr.

PLACE 2
( ) Freddie L. (Fred) Harris
( ) Ernest G. Sansom
( ) Larry Sullivan
( ) E. R. "Gene" Tyson

PLACE 3
( ) Arnold L. Black
( ) Herbert C. Hays
( ) L. J. Keen
( ) John Langham
( ) George Wilmer Moyd

PLACE 4
( ) Frank C. Edmond
( ) W. Leonard Moseley
( ) William A. (Bill) Moser
( ) Felicito (Fleix) Ramos
( ) Shafter Summers

PLACE 5
( ) Norvie Chambers
( ) Roscoe C. Gaillard
( ) Abb Ingram
( ) Don Lyons
( ) Henry M. (Pete) Parker, Jr.
( ) C. D. Saucier
( ) Alford W. Turner

STAND ON KEY ISSUES:

CRIME:

We need a professional police department fully staffed, fully trained, fully equipped, fully paid. We need a department run by a policeman which is polite but efficient, courteous but stern, hardworking and honest.

JOBS AND INDUSTRY:

Prichard must have full employment. I will bring new industry to Prichard. I will bring labor training programs to train people for new jobs. I will appoint a Mayor's Business Advisory Council to assist in getting this job done.

BETTER HOUSING:

In 1972, when men are regularly flying to the moon, it is shameful that human beings have to live in houses like some places in Prichard which simply are not fit for human habitation.

CONCLUSION:

I sincerely ask you to cast your vote on August 8, 1972 for the candidate you feel best qualified to carry this program of progress to save Prichard - cast your vote for the candidate who cares.

A. J. COOPER, JR.

Handbill using campaign themes, reverse side of #3

Jay Cooper

. . . cares about you. Please vote
for him   . . help him
become Mayor of Prichard . . .
help him help you by making
Prichard a better place to live.

SO MUCH NEEDS TO BE DONE

Prichard has many problems . . . big problems. We need more jobs, better housing for many of our people, more parks and playgrounds; too many of our streets are unpaved, poorly lighted, and have open drainage ditches; we are burdened with huge city debt; we need more policemen and they should be better trained and better paid; something needs to be done for people who have to stand hours and hours in long lines for food stamps.

JAY COOPER is the only candidate in the race who cares about all these problems and he is better qualified than any other man in the race to solve them. He will bring government and private money into Prichard which means more jobs and a better life for our people; he will tackle our city's debt problem; see that our streets are paved and that we have more parks and playgrounds; he will improve our police department and he will do something about long food stamp lines.

JAY COOPER believes Prichard can be a wonderful place to live and work. He cares. Help make his dreams come true. Help him become Mayor of Prichard. Vote for Jay Cooper on

VOTE FOR JAY COOPER
Let's Win Without A Runoff

Pd. Pol. Adv. by People for Cooper, W. Pollard, Chmn.

 7

Handbill using campaign themes

Exhibit No. 5

Think About This . . .

Of all the candidates for Mayor of Prichard, Jay Cooper is the only one who can honestly promise to do something about the problems that beset our city. He is the only candidate who knows where to go and how to get government and private funds for municipal improvements, for housing, and for new industry . . . money that would benefit everybody who lives and works in Prichard — black and white, merchant and consumer. Prichard is in trouble. We need a man like Jay Cooper.

Pd. Pol. Adv. by People for Cooper, W. Pollard, Chmn.   7

Handbill for white community

59

Vote to save Prichard

ELECT COOPER

✸ Honesty

✸ Better Law Enforcement

✸ More and Better Jobs

✸ Respect

✸ Better Streets

✸ Decent Housing

Handbill for white community

Tear-off lapel stickers

People for COOPER

Dear Friend:

The New York Times (July 22, 1972) says of the race for Mayor of Prichard, Alabama: Jay Cooper "is favored to win." With just a little more financial help, he can get over the top.

We appeal on behalf of Jay Cooper, the 27-year-old Black lawyer who returned to Alabama to work for Black participation in the politics of his native state. Jay is running for Mayor of Prichard, a suburb of Mobile. A graduate of Notre Dame and New York University Law School, Jay now practices law in Mobile. He is a member of the executive committee of the National Conference of Black Lawyers, was a campaign assistant to the late Robert F. Kennedy and was recipient of a Herbert Lehman Scholarship and an Eleanor Roosevelt Fellowship. Jay returned to private practice and to represent the NAACP Legal Defense Fund in the fight to desegregate southern schools.

Jay has begun an effort to assert a political tradition for a minority that has been without a voice. In Prichard, where no Black candidate has ever run for city office, Jay Cooper is leading a community with an emerging Black majority to fully exercise its political rights.

Jay is also spearheading a drive to register voters who have never used their power at the ballot box. His local support comes from the poorest of a community brought by administrative neglect. We are asking you to help with a contribution.

Contributions totalling $50 per year from a single person or $100 from a couple are tax-deductible, or a tax credit may be claimed on the first $12.50 of a contribution from a single person or $25 from a couple. We hope you will consider this request as a special opportunity to assist not just one man, but to participate in an evolving process of political liberation.

Support the thrust from political apathy to political participation!

Please contribute NOW! Election day is August 8th.

Mail Check to:
PEOPLE FOR COOPER

National fund-raising letter, "People for Cooper" Committee

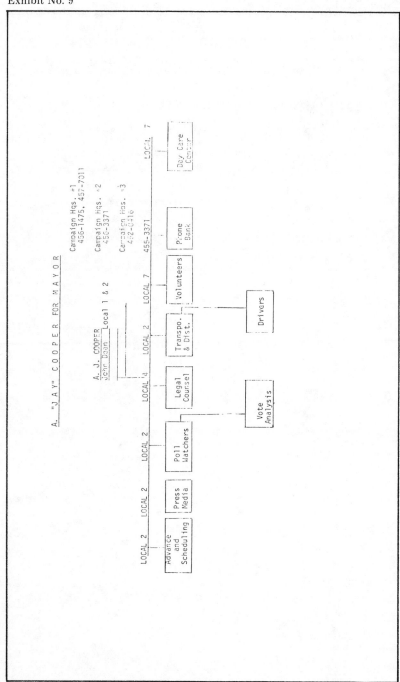

Campaign organization chart

```
A. J. cooper
Political Campaign                              Mobile Office
WGOK RADIO                                      8/5 - 8/7
   30 seconds


HERE'S A TELEPHONE NUMBER TO REMEMBER: 456-3371...CALL 456-3371,

AUGUST 8, ELECTION DAY IN PRICHARD, AND GET A FREE RIDE TO THE

POLLS...AND WHEN YOU GET THERE VOTE FOR JAY COOPER...LET YOUR-

SELF BE HEARD...VOTE...IT'S YOUR SACRED RIGHT AS AN AMERICAN

CITIZEN...VOTE FOR A MAN WHO KNOWS YOUR PROBLEMS AND IS THE ONLY

MAN IN THE RACE QUALIFIED TO SOLVE THEM...SO CALL 456-3371

TUESDAY FOR A RIDE TO THE POLLS...AND VOTE FOR A MAN WHO CARES

...VOTE FOR JAY COOPER.
```

Typical radio spot for ride to polls, 30 seconds

POLL WATCHER'S INSTRUCTION MANUAL

Challengers serve a dual purpose; first, they insure that no election fraud occurs during the balloting; and second, they can keep a running tab of the names of all the registered voters who have voted.

General Poll Watcher Responsibilities

1. To inspect the poll books (but without handling them) as voters names are entered in them.

2. To observe the manner in which the duties of the Election Inspectors are being performed.

3. To challenge the right to vote of anyone whose status as a qualified elector is questionable.

4. To challenge any election procedure that is not being properly performed.

5. To examine the machine totals as they are being counted.

6. To remain at the polling place during the counting of votes and until the returns are duly signed by the Election Inspectors and delivered to the City Clerk.

7. To observe the recording of absentee voters' ballots on voting machines after the close of the polls.

8. To record the names of all the registered voters who have voted.

- - -

Poll watcher's Manual

The law authorized that each candidate can assign one Poll Watcher to each voting machine in each polling place. The Poll Watcher shows his certificate to the Election Inspector upon entering the polling place, must keep it with him at all times and if he leave the polling place must present the certificate again on his return.

Poll Watchers have a right to inspect all operations and procedures which occur at the polling place. They cannot, however, interrupt the flow of voting. If they do so, the Election Inspector of the polling place may have you removed by the police.

Before the polls open, the Poll Watcher should:

1. Arrive at the polling place about 7:30 a.m., before the polling place opens at 8:00 a.m.

2. Check the voting machine number against the number on the envelope which contains the two voting keys. They should be the same.

3. Check the voting machine number against the box number. They should be the same.

4. Check the voting machine number against the number on the voting machine keys. They should be the same.

5. Check the seal number on the voting machine against the number on the envelope which contains the two voting machine keys. They should be the same.

-2-

6. Write down the number which appears in the window of the "Protective Counter". This number represents the total number of times that machine has been voted in all elections in which it has been used.

7. Check the window of the "Public Counter" to be sure that no totals are registered and it reads "0".

To open up voting machine, each machine must be operated by the key with it's number. The wrong number key will not operate the machine.

Steps to operate:

a. Open the front of the machine with key #3

b. Open the top panel at the rear of the machine with key #3

c. Remove the crank in the upper left hand slot at the rear of the machine. Insert the crank in the right hand side of the machine.

d. Turn the crank counter-clock wise until the crank begins to slip. Print-out of the machine ballot will emerge from the back of machine near crank.

e. Slowly pull print-out out of the machine.

f. The print-out should show a "0" total along the right hand column beside the name of each candidate. A certificate appears on the bottom right hand corner of the print-out and wil contain the machine

number. This space will be filled out by the Election
Inspector and attested to by the Poll Watcher assigned
to that machine.

g. The Poll Watcher will not sign this certificate unless
a "0" total appears beside each candidate's name
on the print-out machine ballot.

h. The print-out machine ballot will then be posted in
a convenient place in the polling place for public
view.

i. The seal is removed on the right side of the machine.

j. Key #2 is inserted in machine and turned <u>to point
upward</u>. The key should be taken out of the machine
and the machine is ready for use. "<u>If the key is
not taken out of the machine and someone turns the
key downward, the machine will be out of order for
the whole day</u>". <u>Do not try to lock the top rear
panel after key #2 is turned upward.</u>

k. To use the machine, after the voter enter the curtains, an election official pushes a button on the
outside to close them. When this button is pushed,
<u>one vote must be cast before the machine can be
used again</u>. The voter then pushes a red button
inside the curtains to open them.

l. (For your information) All of the above operating
instructions are located on the left upper rear
portion of the voting machine.

-4-

After the Polls open:

1. Check each voter as he signs in to make sure he is qualified.

2. Make sure that after the voter signs in he does not talk to anyone prior to voting and does not stay too long in the voting booth.

3. Make sure that not voters returns to the polling place after voting.

4. Check the voting machine periodically to insure that the total votes cast corresponds with his own total count.

5. A voter may be assigned by the Election Inspector to vote at a particular machine or if none is assigned he may bot at any machine he wishes.

6. After a voter's name is certified at a particular voting machine, he must vote at that machine.

7. If a voter needs assistance in voting, he may call upon the Election Inspector of that polling place for such assistance or upon any person of his choice.

8. The Election Inspector may assist the voter or he may designate one person for each machine to assist voters at that machine. The Election Inspector and those persons he designates may assist voters during the entire time the polls are open if requested by the individual voter.

9. If the voter, however, chooses the person to assist him, that person must sign a statement and may not assist any other voter that day.

10. When an Election Inspector is assisting a voter, he must render such assistance quickly and immediately leave the booth. He may not designate or suggest any candidate.

11. At each polling place, the chief Poll Watcher will remain at his post all day and will report every hour to headquarters on the running total of votes cast at his polling place and on any general problems or trends. He will also report on voters who support our candidate and who have not yet voted. He will give this information to Ed Anderson who will come by each polling place every hour throughout the day.

CHALLENGING

It is important to challenge a vote only when there is a good reason for challenging. When the Poll Watcher is convinced such a reason exists, he should proceed without hesitation, regardless of any attempt by election officials to discourage him.

1. If the Poll Watcher notices an infraction, he should immediately write down the time, place, names of individuals involved and the nature of the infraction. The Poll Watcher should then tell the Election Inspector of the infraction. If the Poll Watcher is not satisfied with the Election Inspector 's

-6-

action in correcting the infraction,
he must immediately report the incident
in detail by calling   ] or
                at 457-7011 or 456-1475 at
Campaign Headquarters. He will be familiar
with the appropriate section of the Alabama
election law and will take over the protest
at that point.
2. No matter how mad the challenger may be, he
should avoid losing his temper. He should
always be courteous, use a moderate tone of
voice, and not interfere with the Election
Inspector in the proper conduct of his duties.

ELECTION FRAUDS

Here are the most common types of fraud that the challenger

should look out for:

1. Substitute judge or clerk. Forces loyal to our
   opponents may substitute one of their friends
   as a clerk if the regular clerk does not show
   up, check the law to see that proper procedures
   are followed in replacing him (qualified elector
   at ward in question)

2. Jammed or rigged machine. Tampering with machines
   is not very common, but it can occur. The challenger
   should make sure that the "Public Counter" reads
   zero when the day starts and chek the running
   count during the day. If a machine breaks down,
   he should make sure that it is repaired quickly
   (call headquarters if the election officials
   claim they do not have the phone number of the
   firms designated to repair the machines, we
   will have the number.)

3. Vote buying. The transfer of money between individuals either within the polling place or
   near the polls may be a sign that votes are
   being bought.

4. Aid to the handicapped, etc. The law provides
   for assisting the legally handicapped. The
   challenger should make sure that any assistance
   given meets the requirements of the law; that
   the individual who requests the assistance appears
   to need it; and that the person assisting the
   voter does not direct or suggest how the voter
   should vote.

-7-

5. <u>Multiple voting</u>. It is the challenger's job to make sure that a person entering the polling place has not voted before. He should try to remember faces and make sure that the voter does not use false names or credentials.

6. <u>Disqualifying valid voters</u>. There may be attempts to prevent a voter from voting even though he has every legal right. If this occurs, the challenger should have the voter insist on his rights and ask to see the voter registration lists. If he is still not allowed to vote, he should execute a challenged voter oath and have a friend who has known him for at least 2 years prior to the election fill out an identification form.

7. <u>Graveyard voting</u>. This is the tactic of using names of dead or absent voters. The only real way to combat this tactic is to make sure that <u>the list of qualified voters is up to date.</u>

8. <u>Ballot counting fraud</u>. The Poll Watcher should check and recheck to make sure that the total count on each machine adds up to the overall total recorded by the clerk on his talley sheet.

<u>After the polls close, each Poll Watcher should</u>:

1. Check to make sure that the proper officials are present when the machine is opened.

2. Make sure that all those already in line when the polls close have an opportunity to vote.

3. Observe those who are reading the machine or counting ballots to make sure everything is handled properly.

4. Subtract the total now showing in the Protective Counter window from total which showed in that same window when the machine was first opened. (the earlier total should have been recorded by the first Poll Watcher on the shift.) The number arrived at after subtracting these two figures should be the same as that now appearing in the Public Counter window.

-8-

<u>Closing the voting machine</u>:

a. The procedure used to close the machine is the reverse of the one used to open them.

b. Insert key #2 into lock #2 and turn the keys so it is facing down ward. <u>This locks the machine and no more votes can be cast</u>. Poll Watchers will insure that this is done on all machines before leaving their polling places.

c. Open the top panel in the rear of the machine and remove the crank. The crank is then turned clock-wise until it starts to slip. The voting machine print-out in 5 copies will fall out.

d. The totals in the right hand column beside each candidates name from each voting machine in the polling place will be added up and marked beside that candidates name on the single talley sheet of the clerk at the poll. <u>The Poll Watcher is authorized to watch the totaling of the print-out sheets from all of the machines and the entry of the grand total for each candidate on the talley sheet</u>. The Poll Watcher should also add up for himself the total votes for his candidate from each print-out sheet of each voting machine at the polls. If the grand total he gets is not the same as that obtained by the clerk, he should recheck his figures. If they are still not the same, he should call at 457-7011 or 456-1475. If the Election Inspector refuses to have the error corrected in his presence, he should immediately call the lawyers at 457-7011 or 456-1475 and report the names of the officials involved, the time, place and all circumstances surrounding the instance. The lawyers will proceed with the protest from that point on.

e. <u>The Poll Watcher on duty at this time should remain until all of the grand totals are completed</u>, <u>the count has been officially certified by the clerk and copies of each machine print-out and a copy of the grand totals on the talley sheet are posted</u>.

_9_

STATE-REGULATIONS COVERING POLL WATCHERS
CODE OF ALABAMA Recompiled, 1972

(34) <u>Watchers</u> pg. 27

    --must present appointment in writing to inspector
     at assigned polling place

   -- must be sworn in (failthfully observe election laws)

    --may witness opening of voting machine and has
     authority to examine: (1) vote counters to insure
     zero settings; (2) ballots properly placed on machine;
     (3) machine is properly placed (certificate attesting
     to above must be signed by watcher prior to voter
     utilization of machine)

(37) <u>Challenge of Voter</u> pg. 29

    --any person qualified to vote in a particular ward
     can challenge the vote of any person whome he/she
     thinks is not entitled to vote on that ward.

    --a vote challenge must be made to the voting inspector
     <u>before</u> the suspect is permitted to vote.

    --a challenged voter cannot legally vote until he/she
     takes and signs perscribed oath administered by
     voting inspector and has his bona fides sworn by
     another person.

-10-

(38) <u>Voting Procedure When Paper Ballots are Employed</u> pg. 29,30

  --challenger chosen by inspector checks off against

    qualified list of voters and, in absence of challenge,

    clears person to vote

  --each voter gets <u>one</u> ballot with name or initial

    written on stub

  --If voter mismarks or otherwise spoils ballot, it

    may be traded for another (make sure first ballot

    is not later placed in box or recorded)

  --after voting, voter gives folded ballot with stub

    up and vote concealed to inspector who calls out

    voter's name

  --voter's name is entered by vote clerk on "poll list"

    in numerical order

  --voter signs another poll list beside number he was

    assigned on first "poll list."

  --each vote is recorded by number on ballot, and in

    presence of voter number is covered by black seal;

    ballot stub is detached; sealed ballot dropped in

    box.

(41) <u>Number of Electors in Polling Place; Time Limit on</u>

    <u>Occupation of Voting Booth</u> pg. 32

  --using paper ballots-no more than 10 in polling

    place at same time

  --using voting machine - one person per machine

--If other people are waiting to vote, booth or
compartment can only be occupied for 5 minutes--
--If voter fails to vote in 5 minutes he must leave
polling area and cannot legally return.

(43) Counting Votes and Disposition of Poll Lists and
Affidavits When Paper Ballots are Used pg. 33
--both poll lists are placed in separate, labeled,
and sealed envelopes before votes are counted.
--challenged oaths and affidavits shall be packaged
and sealed, with one set to be forwarded to county
grand jury
--votes shall be drawn by inspector or counting
officer one-by-one, and each vote called out loud
enough for bystanders to hear.
--tabulations are compiled separately so that no
recorder is tabulating more than one candidate's
vote

(49) Voter Identification When Voting Machines are Used pg. 36
--voter identifies himself to chief clerk who checks
voter against qualified vote list; if name appears
and voter is unchallenged clerk marks off voter's
name and person votes
--If voter's name does not appear on qualified list
or voter is challenged clerk notifies inspector;
if challenged voter takes oath and obtains witness

-12-

to fill out affidavit for him the challenged voter
can then vote, but only by paper ballot

(104) Closing Polls, Statements Certificates and Returns:
Proclamation of Returns, Disposition of Ballots pg. 70,71
--when polls close voters waiting within polling area
can still vote
--machines are locked immediately after last voter
has voted, and certificated by election officials
(note; certificate states total number of votes
cast on machine, exact time machine was locked and
sealed
--counting compartment is opened in presence of watchers
and representatives of media or associations, if any,
counters numbers shall be placed in full view
--the inspector, under the scrutiny of watchers, calls
out in a loud voice the designating number and letter
(vote totals) on each counter for the candidate's
name; clerk records totals on tally sheet
--the inspector reads-clerk records totals of challenged
ballots cast
--the vote as registered is entered in ink by the
clerk on the "statements of canvas;" entries shall
be made according to machine number
--once filled out, the canvas return is verified so
that it shows the number of votes cast for each
candidate, and is signed by the election officials

-13-

--machine counter compartments remain open while
statements, certificates, and official returns are
compiled and may be inspected by watchers or media
representatives.

--proclaimed vote results for each candidate shall
be announced by the vote inspector

--during the proclamation any person lawfully entitled
to be in the polling place shall be given ample
opportunity to compare the results announced with
the counter dials of the machine and any necessary
corrections shall be made on the spot, after which
the doors of the machine shall be locked and sealed
with the seal provided the election officials.

Exhibit No. 12

WARD 2	BOX	MACHINE NO.	PROTECTIVE CONTROL NO.	PUBLIC COUNTER NO.	SEAL NO.	KEY & ENVELOPE NO.
	1	121260	03847	0	126684	✓
	2	130650	03741	0	126683	✓
	3	130648	03525	0	126682	✓
	4	130651	03834	0	126681	✓
	5	121171	04324	0	126680	✓
	6	130646	03344	0	126679	✓
	7	121257	04856	0	126678	✓
	8	151532	01605	0	126677	✓
	9	151592	01538	0	126676	✓
	10	130643	03582	0	126675	✓
	11	151604	01636	0	126674	✓
	12	121167	03908	0	126673	✓
	13	123830	03419	0	126672	✓
	14	121169	04967	0	126671	✓
	15	151579	01670	0	126670	✓
	16	151612	01630	0	126669	✓
	17	151569	01726	0	126668	✓

The back of the envelope containing the voting machine keys signed by John Dean upon witnessing the sealing of the keys in the envelope.

Voting machine identification data sheet

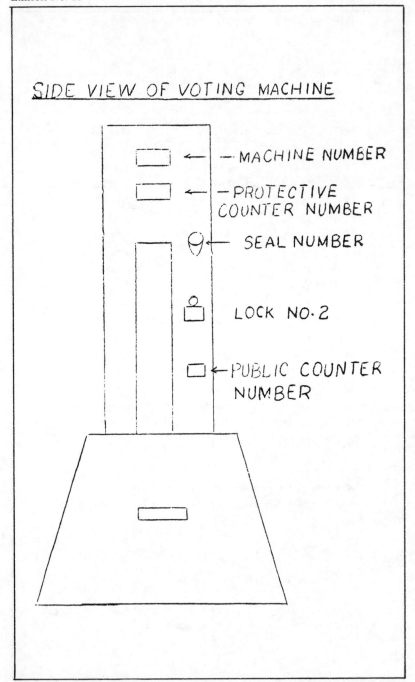

Voting machine diagram

WARD 1-F

Location: Prichard Junior High School

Inspector: Woodrow W. Donald   Timothy-Prichard

No 1 Machine:

Chief Clerk, Martha Floyce McKee; Assistant Clerk, Idouma L. Havard; Assistant Clerk, Mrs. Marguerite Cave.

No 2 Machine:

Clerk, Curtis C. Boutwell; Clerk, Ruby Kennedy; Clerk, E. F. Eubanks.

No 3 Machine:

Clerk, Venna Knowles Curtis; Clerk, Evelyn F. Armstrong; Clerk, Mazie White Wiggins.

No 4 Machine:

Clerk, Myrtie L. Swendull; Clerk, Dorothy P. Williams; Clerk, Owen Wood.

No 5 Machine:

Clerk, Hessie Bell Rutherford; Clerk, Mrs. Willis Hearnden; Clerk, Virgil Fred Gardner.

No 6 Machine:

Clerk, Ada Brown Persons; Clerk, Irene Waller; Clerk, Ruby Eone Donald.

No 7 Machine:

Clerk, Gritie Mae Hiatt; Clerk, Nell E. Dudley; Clerk, Woodrow Langley.

No 8 Machine:

Clerk, Kitty Sue Englebert; Clerk, A. L. Galson; Clerk, Lelia G. Taylor.

List of ward election officials (one prepared for each ward)

POLL WATCHER _____

WARD Nº. _____

MACHINE Nº. _____

TOTALS AT CLOSE OF POLLS:

POLL WATCHERS RECORD TOTALS FOR EACH CANDIDATE

Capps	Cooper	Jacobson	McNorton	Phillips	Sanders	Turner

POLL WATCHERS RECORD THE ABOVE INFORMATION FROM THE TALLEY SHEET WHEN YOUR MACHINE IS CLOSED. GIVE TO COOPER CHIEF WATCHER.

CHIEF POLL WATCHERS MUST USE THIS FORM TO RECORD AND REPORT THE FINAL TOTAL OF ALL VOTES CAST IN THAT WARD FOR OUR CANDIDATE. THE TOTAL OF ALL MACHINES FOR EACH CANDIDATE SHOULD BE ADDED AND PLACED IN THE APPROPRIATE BOX ABOVE. YOUR TOTALS MUST EQUAL THE TOTAL RECORDED BY THE ELECTION OFFICIAL ON THE OFFICIAL WARD TALLEY SHEET.

DO NOT LEAVE THE POLLING PLACE UNTIL YOU ARE SURE ALL TOTALS ARE ACCURATE AND MACHINES PROPERLY LOCKED.

CALL HEADQUARTERS = 457-7011 OR 456-1475 WITH YOUR TOTALS.

Vote tally sheet (one prepared for each voting machine)

Together We Can SAVE PRICHARD!

Corruption and inefficiency have driven the City of Prichard to the point of bankruptcy.

Don't be fooled anymore. Don't let politicans keep building smoke screens of racial divisions to hide their lack of leadership.

A.J. Cooper can work with white and black people to save Prichard for all of us.

We all want the same good city services we deserve for our tax money.

Let's get behind Cooper and start moving Prichard ahead.

Because We're ALL In This Together!
A.J. "JAY" COOPER

Pd. Pol. Adv. By A.J. Cooper

New handbills with new themes

Together We Can SAVE PRICHARD!

Prichard is dying.

Four more years of corruption and inefficiency will finish us off.

Imagine--the sixth largest city in Alabama with one of the largest work forces in the South--BANKRUPT!

Hardworking men and women, white and black, paying their taxes and letting their city go down the drain!

Don't let politicans divide us by racial hatred while they plunder the city.

COOPER will work with white and black to KEEP PRICHARD ALIVE FOR US ALL.

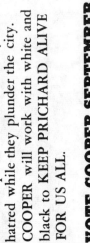

VOTE COOPER SEPTEMBER 12

A.J. "JAY" COOPER

(Pd. Pol. Adv. By A.J. Cooper)

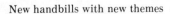

New handbills with new themes

1 + **One** = **2**
2 + **One** = **3**
3 + **One** = **4**
4 + **One** = **5**
5 + **One** = **6**
6 + **One** = **7**
7 + **One** = **Your Vote Counts!**

Jay Cooper needs your vote so Prichard can have a good and well-qualified mayor.

You may be the One to put him there.

Vote Sept. 12 for "JAY" COOPER!

Pd. Pol. Adv. By A.J. Cooper   38

New handbills with new themes

Together We Can SAVE PRICHARD!

TO THE WHITE VOTERS OF PRICHARD:

I ask your support in the September 12 runoff for mayor on my qualifications and on my pledge to work for all the people of Prichard . . . white and black.

Our city faces a crisis. Not of race relations. Not of whether we shall have black or white city officials. We face a crisis of whether we shall have a city for anyone to govern. Or enjoy.

We face a crisis of whether the state's sixth largest city will go down the drain in bankruptcy without adequate city services or police protection.

That is why 77% of the voters August 8 voted against the incumbent mayor.

I will use my legal training and experience to put Prichard on a sound financial basis, to obtain for our taxpayers all the federal funds to which we are entitled, to use them properly, and to give all our people, white and black, the best city services possible.

Together, we can make Prichard a city of pride. Divided by race, we will sit back and see it decay.

A.J. COOPER

Pd. Pol Adv. By A.J. Cooper

New handbill for white community

Cooper for Mayor Headquarters
553 Wilson Avenue
Prichard, Alabama 36610

Dear   :

    I imagine my friend   has already spoken to you about
my candidacy for Mayor of Prichard, Alabama and the primary election that
was recently held on August 8th. In that primary we achieved a number of
unprecedented gains. We brought out the largest turn-out of voters in the
history of Prichard, received the largest vote of any black man ever to
run for Mayor in the state of Alabama and the largest number of votes ever
received by a black man running for elective office in Prichard. In a field
with six white candidates, one of whom was a 12-year incumbent, I still received over 45% of the votes in one of the strongest Wallace areas of the
state.

    Unfortunately, because of my percentage of the vote, I now face a run-
off election on September 12th. I am bringing together again the same team
of national black political experts and local leaders and supporters who
performed so magnificently for me in August. I would like to call on you
for a contribution. Please send it to People for Cooper at the above address.

    Because of your record hits, you have many friends in Prichard. It
would be of enormous help to me if you would tape a recording of support
for me. I have taken the liberty of enclosing a suggested script to which
you can dub in your own background music.

    Please help us continue what we have already proven we can do, change
the city of Prichard from a community of political apathy to a community of
political participation.

    I need your help.

Sincerely,

A. "Jay" Cooper

Typical letter to black entertainers with attached radio spot script

Hi, this is   asking   in
Prichard, Alabama. Is there enough love to elect Jay Cooper for Mayor
in the run-off election on September 12th. He is a man who truly cares
about the people and problems of Prichard. A man who knows of the need
for more jobs, good health care, and better housing for all the citizens.
Jay Cooper is the only candidate who knows where to go and how to get
government and private funds to make Prichard a wonderful place to live
and work.

I urge all of my friends to register now and vote on September 12th.

Yes, I believe there is enough love in Prichard to help Jay Cooper
help you make Prichard a better place to live. Save Prichard, Vote for
Jay Cooper on September 12th.

Hi, this is   . In my record, _____
I sing about the mood and condition of that unusual part of town. I was
born in a ghetto and I know what it's like to live there. A lot of people
think ghettos are only where black people live, but ghettos are where poor
people live, whether they are black or white. There are a lot of ghettos
in Prichard, Alabama, but you don't have to have them. Vote for Jay Cooper
for Mayor in the September 12th run-off election. He knows where to attract the money that will benefit everybody who lives and works in Prichard.
Save Prichard. Vote for Jay Cooper for Mayor on September 12th.

This is Senator_____.

I am taking this opportunity to speak to you on behalf of my friend, Jay Cooper because I share the concern of the citizens of Prichard, Alabama who wish to live in an economically prosperous city free from over-burdening debt. I share your desire to realize the great potential of your city; to have full employment, decent nousing, good medical care, paved, safe streets, and a healthy environment for all who live and work in Prichard.

Turning these desires into reality will require that you exercise the most precious right that you have as an American citizen; the right to vote. I urge those of you who have not done so to register now so that you can vote in the September 12th run-off election. I urge you also to Save Prichard and vote on September 12th for the man who knows your problems and is best qualified to solve them. Vote for Jay Cooper.

Radio spot script for U.S. Senator

Cooper for Mayor Headquarters
553 South Wilson Avenue
Prichard, Alabama 36610
August 18, 1972

Dear Friend:

The August 9th issue of the "Washington Post," states, "Algernon J. 'Jay' Cooper, posted the most impressive win ever for a black candidate for mayor in a major Alabama city." This "Impressive" win must be shared with all the people.

Throughout the campaign, "Jay" Cooper has addressed the issues facing the majority of the people who live in Prichard. He has taken a firm stand on many issues including food stamps and housing. Over 65% of the people of Prichard live in dilapidated housing. Food stamp recipients must stand in long unnecessary lines before receiving their stamps. "Jay" Cooper, will take positive steps to end these problems; he will bring Prichard to its fullest potential.

We have used new media techniques - which have never been used by a black candidate in a municipal election - to reach the people, enabling us to attain these goals.

We need your help in keeping such an aggressive and informative campaign moving. A victory on September 12th, means progress for Prichard, and its surrounding areas. We must join "Jay" Cooper, and make this happen. If we do, we join thousands of people in the city of Prichard who are determined to bring about a change.

In order for us to effect this change, we will need the help of civic minded people in southern Alabama. We are soliciting your financial assistance in our campaign to make Prichard a safe and happy place to live.

Yours for a progressive Prichard,

Coordinators,
"100 Women For Cooper"

Local fund-raising letter, Women for Cooper organization

100 WOMEN FOR COOPER

Please make checks payable to "People for Cooper."

Your contribution is tax deductible. Effective January 1, 1972, you may take a tax deduction for contributions to the Cooper for Mayor Funf. Political contributions up to $100.00, during 1972 may be deducted by a married couple filing a joint return. Contributions up to $50.00 may be deducted by a single person . (or a married person filing separately.)

Alternately, you may take a tax credit for one half of your political contributions during 1972.

A credit up to $25.00 may be taken by a married couple. A credit up to $12.50, may be taken by a single person (or a married person filing separately.)

Cooper for Mayor Headquarters
553 Wilson Avenue
Prichard, Alabama 36610

Dear

 This letter is pursuant to the phone conversation I had with you today.
I most urgently need any assistance you can give me and I am particularly in
need of financial contributions at this point in the campaign to insure that
I will have the necessary election day workers on which the outcome could very
well depend.

 As you may know, in the primary which was held on August 8th we achieved
a number of unprecedented gains. We brought out the largest turn-out of voters
in the history of Prichard, received the largest vote of any black man ever to
run for Mayor in the state of Alabama, and the largest number of votes ever received by a black man running for elective office in Prichard. In a field with
six white candidates, one of whom was a 12-year incumbent, I still received over
45% of the votes in one of the strongest Wallace areas of the state.

 Because of my percentage of the vote, I now face a run-off election on
September 12th. I am bringing together again the same team of national black
political experts and local leaders and supporters who performed so magnifi-
cantly for me in August. Would you please send a contribution to the above
address and help us continue what we have already proven we can do, change the
city of Prichard from a community of political apathy to a community of political participation.

 I need your help.

Sincerely,

A. "Jay" Cooper

Typical individual letter to potential contributors

Dear Women For Cooper:

The Jay Cooper Campaign is sponsoring a Nickel and Dime Campaign on the 9th of September beginning at 8:30 A.M. and ending 6:30 P.M. This campaign is being sponsored for two reasons:

1. To mobilize all of the young people of Prichard and get them active in the political process that control their lives by going door to door and having one to two minute seminars with the citizens of Prichard informing them of Mr. Cooper's stand on the many key issues that press all of us, young and old, rich and poor, black and white and what kind of programs that the candidate has devised to deal with the many problems affecting the City of Prichard.

2. Realizing that the City of Prichard is a very poor community, and many citizens would like to contribute to the Cooper Campaign but don't have the Dollars that it takes to obtain good government and have good leadership we are asking all of us to pool together our nickels and dimes in an effort to raise the necessary Dollars to insure good government within the City of Prichard.

All monies raised will go toward Mr. Cooper's expenses incurred during the primary and the up coming run-off on September 12th.

What You Can Do

We are in need of 300 students that will come from all walks of life within the City of Prichard. We are in hopes that you will allow your teen-ager to participate. The students will be well supervised by adults that will be working as Captains and Monitors of the Nickel and Dime Campaign. We need to know the number of young people that will be participating from your household by September 1.

Please have all your students attend briefing September 6, 1972 at 7:30 P.M. or you may call 452-0416 or 456-1475 and ask to speak with Alberta Richardson or leave the message as to the name, telephone number and address of your young participant.

If you are anyone you know is a sponsor of an organization and that organization would like to enter the Nickel and Dime Campaign there will be three throphys awarded. 1st prize will

Letter to Women for Cooper organization on nickel and dime campaign

go to the organization that collects the most money and pass
out the most literature; 2nd prize will go to the organization
with the largest number of participants; 3rd prize will go to the
organization that collects the most money with the smallest number
of participants. These throphys are beautiful in design and
would be quite a prize for Baptist Training Union, Junior
Choir, the Cub Scouts and any other youth organization that
you are someone you know may sponsor.

We hope that we can all band together in this all out
effort for better government within our city.

Looking forward to hearing from you.

                                    Chairman
                                    Nickel and Dime Campaign

P.S. Please give these 10 leaflets to 10 young people on your
      street.

HEY BROTHERS AND SISTERS
COME JOIN THE NICKEL AND DIME CAMPAIGN!!!

DATE - SEPTEMBER 9, 1972

TIME - 8;30 A.M.

PLACE- COOPER HEADQUARTERS # 1
926 St. Stephens Road

WE NEED BLACK LEADERSHIP IN PRICHARD—A BLACK
MAYOR AND SOME BLACK CITY COUNCILMEN. IF WE
ARE TO GET THIS CANDIDATE ELECTED, WE NEED
YOUR HELP.

MR. COOPER, CANDIDATE FOR MAYOR, NEED 350
STUDENTS TO CARRY LITERATURE-COLLECT NICKELS
AND DIMES - QUARTERS AND FIFTY CENTS FROM ALL
OF THE BROTHERS AND SISTERS OF PRICHARD SO THAT
WE WILL HAVE THE FINANCE TO MAKE SEPTEMBER 12,
1972 A SWEET VICTORY FOR ALL OF THE PEOPLE
IN PRICHARD AND THIS INCLUDES YOU, THE YOUTH.
IF YOU WOULD LIKE TO PARTICIPATE IN THIS
CAMPAIGN, PLEASE BE AT

COOPER HEADQUARTERS
September 6 — 7:30 P.M.

FOR A BRIEFING AND ALL OF THE FACTS............

NICKEL AND DIME COMMITTEE FOR BLACK LEADERSHIP

CHAIRMAN

Immediate Things Needed to Conduct the Nickel and Dime Campaign

1. Letters to
   150 Women For Cooper soliciting their teen-agers involvement.
   Student Body Presidents of Blount and Vigor
   BTU Sponsors of each Baptist Church located in Prichard
   Other youth groups.

2. Materials and Supplies
   300 bumper stickers
   300 beer cans
   paper hats
   500 envelopes
   1 ream memo paper
   500 stamps

3. Personnel
   300 participants
   30 adults (to serve as Monitors or Captains)
   2 telephone co-ordinators
   2 Registrars
   8 Drivers

4. Transportation for all participants.

5. Meetings that need to take place before the 8th and 9th.
   8/23/72 - Meet with all of the young people involved in the campaign now.
   8/29/72 - Meet with the 30 monitors, drivers, registrars and telephone
             coordinators
   9/1/72 - Meet with all personnel involved for progress and briefing.
   9/6/72 - Meet with all 300 participants and supervisory personnel.

6. Assignments that must be made immediately

   1. Donated items such as beer cans, bumper stickers and hats.
   2. Securing the 30 monitors and student leaders
   3. Securing meeting places and transportation as well as drivers
   4. Write letters, news releases and any other media coordination.
   5. Over-all coordinator. This should be someone that can tie down
      loose ends of step 1 thru 4 and has absolute time to devote.
   6. Someone to zone off the different communities using the City of
      Prichard Map and make assignments by street, intersections and
      shopping centers (suggest Mrs.

Internal staff planning documents on nickel and dime campaign

NICKEL AND DIME CAMPAIGN FOR JAY COOPER

September 1972

The purpose of the Nickel and Dime campaign is to let every person within the City of Prichard contribute to the election of the new Mayor of Prichard. Realizing that Prichard is a very poor city and everybody cannot afford to give dollars, but that everyone would like to contribute to the campaign, we intend to go out into the streets and solicit nickels, dimes and quarters, or whatever a person can afford to contribute. By doing this, each person contributing their nickel or dime would more likely remember on election day that he or she has money invested in the Cooper Campaign; therefore, casting their vote for the election of Jay Cooper, for Mayor of Prichard.

This campaign will have a two-phase purpose. The other phase will be to get in the hands of everybody contributing to the campaign, literature on the stands, platform and other needed information about the candidate. Each person participating in the Nickel and Dime C...... should have in his or her possession literature to pass out, some type of identification that would identify Jay Cooper on sight and be well versed so that they will be able to carry on a one or two minute conversation about the candidate to the person contributing.

Material and Personnel Needed

Looking at all of the communities that have to be visited, the main intersections, stores and shopping centers, teen-age gatherings, we need to mobilize a minimum of 300 participants. Each participant needs:

1. beer can with a bumper sticker wrapped around it stating ,"Elect Jay Cooper "
2. 1 hat (If possible ready made donated hats, if not, home made hats) with the word COOPER boldly printed on it
3. 1 arm band with the name COOPER in bold letters
4. Enough literature so that one could spend a full day in the field passing out literature as they collect the nickels and dimes.
5. A large enough building where 300 students and 30 monitors or captains can meet and be briefed on the need, the purpose and the candidate.

All volunteers will meet on September 6 at 6:30 p.m. and will be briefed on the procedures of the nickel and dime campaign, the community they will be in charge of, the shopping centers, the main intersections and to insure that they have all of the needed supplies in order to conduct the campaign. This will include transportation to get the students to their particular assignments.

Key Areas in Communities and Streets and Shopping Centers that Should Be Hit.

A. Shopping Centers

Beltline Shopping Center	5 members
Longs Grocery	4 Members
Freemans Grocery	4 members
Save More Shopping Center	8 members (2 per building)
Down Town Prichard	15 members equally divided into 3 sections and blocks
8 Mile Shopping Center	6 members (if possible all white)
Whistler Shopping Center	5 members (an integrated group)
Krystal's on Whistler Ave.	4 members (2 white and 2 black)
45 Strip	7 members

Internal staff planning documents on nickel and dime campaign

Intersections
These are some of the main intersections that will be visited.

1.	The Y in Toulminville	6 members minimum
2.	Prichard Lane & 45	4 members
3.	45 & 1st Avenue	2 members
4.	Prichard Lane & Wilson Ave.	4 members
5	Prichard Lane & Craft Highway	2 members
6.	Bay Bridge & Telegraph Rd.	4 members

Meet with the rest of the staff in picking out the main intersections in Whistler, Chickasaw Terrace and any other community that has been left out. This could be the function of the 30 monitors or captains to decide the rest of the intersection.

COMMUNITIES
The rest of the students that are not accounted for should be assigned to go door to door. They will be briefed in the need of being courteous, how to conduct a one to two minute conversation with the resident of the home about the canadidate.
Communities that must be visited are as follows:
1. The community bounded by Whistler Avenue parallel with Owens Street bounded by Berkley Avenue and Sweeney"s Lane.
2. Chickasaw Terrace
3. Whistler
4. Alexander Court
5. Joel Court (to include the New Prichard Housing Project across the street)
6. Bessemer Street Apartments
7. Snug Harbor and any other heavily populated community omitted from this document.

WAYS OF RECRUITING PARTICIPANTS
Since we are talking about conducting the Nickel and Dime Campaign after school starts, one of the ways we can recruit young people is to now start identifying student leaders at Blount Prichard Middle School and Vigor and recruit from the contacts that they give us; utilize the existing young staff members to recruit their friends; start announcing on the radio requesting young people to participate in the Nickel and Dime Campaign.

THE MONITORS RESPONSIBILITIES
Each monitor will be assigned to coordinate and be responsible for 30 students. The Nickel and Dime Campaign will be divided into 30 sections and 30 components. Each monitor will be assigned to 1 section and 1 component. Their job will be to check with the students and insure that all students are on their particular sites; brief all participants about the Nickel and Dime Campaign; finally to collect and count all monies collected by the participants.

A. "JAY" COOPER FOR MAYOR CAMPAIGN

A. "JAY" COOPER
JOHN DEAN, CAMPAIGN MANAGER

HEADQUARTERS NUMBER I	HEADQUARTERS NUMBER III	HEADQUARTERS NUMBER II
926 St. Stephens Road 457-7011	553 So. Wilson Ave. 452-0416, 455-1475	603 South Wilson Ave. 455-3371
Headquarters Directors:	Office Manager:	Headquarters Directors:
	Poll Watchers:	
	Advance Scheduling:	
Literature:		Get-Out-The-Vote:
Distribution:	Transportation:	Volunteers
	Community Organization:(Whistler,	Voter Registration:
Nickel and Dime:	8 Mile and Ward I)	
Legal Counsel:		
	Coordinator:	
	Press:	

Campaign organizational chart

A. "JAY" COOPER FOR MAYOR CAMPAIGN

SCHEDULE

DATE: August 20th

8:00 _____

9:00 _____

10:00 _____

11:15 Arrive New Holmes Baptist Church-Jay
11:00 _____
11:30 Speak New Holmes Baptist Church -Jay

12:00 Rev. Boykin's Church, Central Baptist- Jay speak

1:00 _____

2:00 _____

3:00 Mt. Carmel Baptist Church- Jay speak

4:00 _____

5:00 Alex Douglass; Cliff Howard, meeting

6:00 _____

7:00 Elks meeting-Club Harlem-Dean speaks

7:30 Gospel Program ILA Hall- Jay speak
8:00 _____

9:00 _____

10:00 _____

Typical daily schedule for the candidate

Speaking Outline

I. Urge non-registered persons to register to vote as soon as possible (Use information contained in "How to Register to Vote" information sheet.)

II. Give essential points on how to get an application for an Absentee ballot (use information contained in "Instruction for Getting out an application for an Absentee Ballot by mail".)

III. Stress the critical need for volunteers to be Poll Watchers and Drivers on election day, September 12th. (Get their names and phone numbers)

IV. Stress the importance of voting on September 12th for Jay Cooper, John Langham, Fred Harris and Reverend Handy Davis. (Give number 456-3371 to call for ride to poll.)

Speaker's outline for Women for Cooper church addresses

CENTRAL
CENTRAL BAPTIST CHURCH

Rev. L. Boykin, Pastor

7:30 p.m.   August 29, 1972

"INVOLVEMENT"

DEVOTION   Mrs. Inez G. Lawson

WELCOME   Mrs. C.P. Williams

RESPONSE   Mrs. Yancina Douglas

OCCASION   Mrs. L.W. Portis

    ROLE OF THE CHURCH IN POLITICS   Mrs. Lonia M. Gill

    ROLE OF THE COMMUNITY IN POLITICS   Mrs. Juanita Mickles

    ROLE OF BUSINESS IN POLITICS   Mrs. Lucinda Portis

    ROLE OF THE SCHOOL IN POLITICS   Mrs. Ruth Collins

ECHOES FROM THE CANDIDATES

    HANDY DAVIS................. Candidate for Place # 1

    FREDDIE HARRIS.............. Candidate for Place # 2

    JOHN LANGHAM............... Candidate for Place # 3

    A."JAY" COOPER.............. Candidate for Mayor

COMMITMENTS OF INVOLVEMENTS TO CANDIDATES   John Dean

QUESTION AND ANSWER PERIOD   (All Candidates)   John Dean

REMARKS

BENEDICTION

Women for Cooper program for all black candidates

103

Exhibit No. 31

```
┌─────────────────────────────────────────────────────────────────────────┐
│                                                                           │
│                A."JAY" COOPER FOR MAYOR CAMPAIGN                           │
│                      Schedule         Friday, August 25, 1972             │
│                VICE MAYOR MAYNARD JACKSON'S VISIT                          │
│                                                                           │
│  3:30 -  Party assembles for ride to airport at Headquarters III.         │
│                                                                           │
│  3:45 -  Party departs for airport                                        │
│                                                                           │
│  4:55 -  Vice Mayor Jackson arrives N.A. #474                             │
│                                                                           │
│  5:30 -  Party arrives Malaga Inn -  Rest period                          │
│                                                                           │
│  6:15 -  Party departs Malaga Inn for shopping center tour                │
│                                                                           │
│  6:30 -  Party arrives SaveMore Store, 911 S. Wilson Ave. (Contact        │
│          Mr. Perry)                                                        │
│                                                                           │
│  6:45 -  Party departs Save More                                          │
│                                                                           │
│  6:50 -  Party arrives  TG&Y Store at Beltline Shopping Center            │
│          (Contact                                                         │
│                                                                           │
│  7:10 -  Party departs TG&Y Store. Cars #1 and #5 proceed to WALA -       │
│          TV  for 8 minute taping session.  Cars #2,3 and 4 proceed        │
│          to P.O.W. rally                                                   │
│                                                                           │
│  8:00 -  Party departs WALA - TV                                          │
│                                                                           │
│  8:25 -  Party arrives Home Street Baptist Church, 815 Max St. for        │
│          P.O.W. sponsored rally   Rev. Hatcher  (Contact Nick Solomon)    │
│                                                                           │
│  9:55 -  Party departs rally                                              │
│                                                                           │
│  10:00 - Party arrives Phillips Temple, AOH, St. Stephens Rd.             │
│          Bishop Phillips  (contact Irene Ware)                            │
│                                                                           │
│  10:25 - Party departs Phillips Temple                                    │
│                                                                           │
│  10:30 - Party arrives M&M Auditorium, 957 Spring Hill Ave.  Benefit      │
│          Cabaret for Roger Williams Community center  (contact Melvin     │
│          West)       ................                                      │
│                                Saturday August 26, 1972                    │
│                                                                           │
│  9:00 -  Party departs Malaga Inn for Headquarters III                    │
│                                                                           │
│  9:30 -  Joint press conference, Vice Mayor Maynard Jackson and           │
│          A."Jay" Cooper                                                    │
│  10:00 - Party departs for Discount Food Store, 732 W. Main Street        │
│                                                                           │
│  10:30 - Party departs store                                              │
│                                                                           │
│  10:30 - 11:30 - Rest period at Headquarters III                          │
│                                                                           │
│  11:30 - Party departs for airport                                        │
│                                                                           │
│  12:00 - Party arrives at airport                                         │
│                                                                           │
│  12:20 - Vice Mayor Jackson departs Mobile                                │
│                                                                           │
│                                Campaign Manager - John Dean               │
│                                                                           │
└─────────────────────────────────────────────────────────────────────────┘
```

Example of schedule for black dignitary (Vice Mayor Maynard Jackson)

104

CEDAR GROVE BAPTIST CHURCH

8:00 p.m.   Rev. Percy Ely, Pastor   September 11, 1972

INVOCATION

PRAYER AND SCRIPTURE   Rev. Handy L. Davis

WELCOME   Rev. Percy Ely

INSTRUMENTAL SOLO   Mrs. Susie Guy

INTRODUCTION OF MAYOR HATCHER   Hawk Ephraim Sr.

SPEAKER   RICHARD GORDON HATCHER, MAYOR
                                                 GARY, INDIANA

A + B SELECTION

                              OFFERING

INTRODUCTION OF REV. RALPH ABERNATHY   Nick Solomon, President
                                                        P.O.W.

SPEAKER   REV. RALPH DAVID ABERNATHY, PRESIDENT
                                                 SOUTHERN CHRISTIAN LEADERSHIP
                                                 CONFERENCE (SCLC)

REMARKS   A."JAY" COOPER, CANDIDATE FOR MAYOR OF PRICHARD

               HANDY DAVIS, CANDIDATE FOR PLACE # I

               FRED HARRIS, CANDIDATE FOR PLACE # II

               JOHN LANGHAM, CANDIDATE FOR PLACE # III

REMARKS AND BENEDICTION   Rev. Percy Ely

_____

              Mistress of Ceremony - Mrs. L. B. Stewart

Example of programmed event for black dignitary (Mayor Richard Hatcher
and Rev. Ralph Abernathy)

Thank You Sincerely . . .

. . . For the strong vote you gave me on August 8th. Please vote for me again September 12th. I promise if I am elected mayor of Prichard I will dedicate myself whole-heartedly to making Prichard a better place for everybody who lives and works here. I promise to work with all the people of Prichard on our economic problems, to make Prichard a better place for our youth, to solve our transportation and health and sanitation problems and to solve the city's debt problem. So much needs to be done. And it can be done if the black and white citizens of Prichard work together. Thank you again for the votes I received August 8th; and again I ask you to vote for me September 12th.

Jay Cooper

Typical newspaper ad urging run-off support

Exhibit No. 34

COOPER FOR MAYOR HEADQUARTERS
AUGUST 21, 1972

News Release

The Honorable Maynard Jackson, Vice Mayor of Atlanta, Georgia, will arrive
on this Friday, August 25th to campaign for A. "Jay" Cooper who is a candidate
for Mayor of Prichard.

A prominent leader and national spokesman on problems of city government,
Vice Mayor Jackson will tour a number of local shopping centers in the early
evening on Friday with Cooper.

Both will also appear at a free public rally at Rev. T. J. Batcher's
Holmes Street Baptist Church, Friday, August 25 at 8:00 p.m., according to
Nick Soloman, president of Workers of Prichard.

In commenting on his campaigning in behalf of Cooper, Jackson said, "I
have personally known Jay for a number of years and I believe he is without
doubt one of the most qualified young men I know running for elective office
today.

"I sincerely beleive that with his national contacts in industry and government, he will be able to obtain the necessary financial resources to get Prichard on the move."

The two political leaders will hold a joint press conference Saturday morning, August 26th at 9:30 a.m. at Cooper's campaign headquarters #3, 553 S. Wilson
Avenue.

Vice Mayor Jackson is the recipient of a number of national awards and hon-
ors. He is a member of the American Bar Association, the National Bar Association,
the Policy Council of the Democratic National Committee and the National League of
Cities.

Example of news release for black dignitary (Vice Mayor Maynard Jackson)

Exhibit No. 35

PRESS   RELEASE

Cooper Campaign Headquarters   September 5, 1972

Prichard, Alabama is facing a crisis. My opponent is trying to get people
to believe that the crisis is about being white or black. The truth is that
he is just building a smoke screen to hide behind. Vernon Capps is directly
responsible for the crisis in Prichard in a number of areas. However, there
is no area more important than law enforcement. Vernon Capps has been coddling
the criminals and holding hands with the crooks of this town.

Our police bring people in one door and Capps lets them out the back door. We
will never have a decent city if the Mayor does not support the police. As
dope pushers are coming more and more into Prichard we don't need a man who has
granted extension of time to 2,280 people convicted of crime. But while the
City was losing a total of $64,921, as a result of this practice, the Mayor
himself directly caused the city to lose $19,791, from fines he gave criminals
time to pay.

I have revealed my income tax return. I again demand that Vernon Capps reveal
his income tax returns for every year he has been in office. The people deserve
to know. The people who had to be laid off because of a lack of money want to
know. The police who risk their lives night and day deserve to know.

I believe that there is no authority for the mayor to give people time to pay
and thus he is violating the law. When I am elected, I will ask the legislature
to repeal the authority given to remit fines, and I will ask the District Attorney and Attorney General to recover the fines illegally continued.

for further information:

456-1475
452-0416

Typical news release attacking incumbent on faulty administrative practices

Fool me once, shame on you. Fool me twice, shame on me.

Mayor Vernon Capps has been fooling the people of Prichard for 12 years, and every year the city has gotten into worse shape than it was the year before. Prichard is dangerously in debt; there is even talk of bankruptcy. Garbage collection and other municipal services are very poor, to say the least. Crime increases, and the mayor does nothing to stop it! Too many streets are unpaved, and paved streets are cracked and broken. Drainage ditches are filled with weeds and stagnant water. City government has broken down. As another candidate in the August 8 primary pointed out . . . "we know that Prichard's biggest problem is Mayor Vernon Capps himself . . ."

Mayor Capps wants to blame the city council for his own failures and the sorry condition of our city. He can't do that!

We've been fooled enough. Twelve years is too long to put up with the kind of government Mayor Capps has given us.

It's time we had an educated, concerned young man in the mayor's office who will give Prichard the able leadership we need to rebuild our city. We need A. "Jay" Cooper, Jr., in the Mayor's office. He is a lawyer, and a man of proven integrity, and proven ability and leadership. He has proven that he is fair minded, and that he is concerned over the welfare of our city. Jay Cooper knows where to go and how to get government and private funds to rebuild Prichard. He will work with all the people of Prichard, both black and white, to build a city we can all be proud of. We need Jay Cooper in the mayor's office, because together we can save Prichard.

ELECT JAY COOPER
MAYOR OF PRICHARD!!

Pd. Pol. Adv. by People for Cooper, W. Pollard, Chairman

Typical newspaper ad attacking incumbent's general administration

Here is something for the people of Prichard to think
about: Jay Cooper can honestly promise to do something
about the problems that beset Prichard. He knows where
to go and how to get federal and private funds for municipal improvements, for housing, and new industry...money
to benefit everybody who lives in Prichard...black and
white...merchant and consumer. Together we can save
Prichard. A vote for Jay Cooper for mayor is a vote
for yourself and your family.

This has been a paid political advertisement by People
for Cooper, W. Pollard, Chairman.

Typical radio spot urging run-off support and ride to polls, 30 seconds

Exhibit No. 38

Volunteer Promo

I am urging students of the Prichard area to come out at 7:00 p.m. on Wed., Sept. 6, 1972 to the Cooper Headquarters #1 at 926 St. Stephens Rd., and help me to save Prichard. We are going to be knocking on doors and passing out literature to everyone. We need your help to bring a program to save Prichard to the people.

Come out tonight and every afternoon after school at 1:00 p.m. to help us save Prichard.

We are raffling off tickets to the   Show at the Municipal Auditorium on Sept. 14, for participants in our campaign. Come out and help us to save Prichard. Whether Prichard lives or dies depends on whether you care.

Radio spot requesting student volunteers, 15 seconds

111

VOLUNTEERS NEEDED

Headquarters NO. I

1. Receptionist-Coordinator- two young adults, one for morning and afternoon shift.

2. Canvassing and literature distribution supervisor- six, for morning and afternoon shifts.

Headquarters NO. II.

1. Drivers to take people to register- six, for morning and afternoon shifts

2. Counters for registration office- two, for morning and afternoon shifts

3. Coordinators and Community contact People for registration drive, four same.

4. Phone Bank Volunteers- 18, for morning and afternoon shifts.

Headquarters NO. III.

1. Receptionsist- Office Coordinator- two young adults, one for morning and afternoon shift.

2. Assistant Office Manager- 1 full time, if possible or 2 persons for shifts.

3. Typists - two, one for morning and afternoon shift.

4. Campaign Activities and Schedule Coordinators - four, two to work on alternate days, if you cannot get 2 to work full time.

Outline of volunteer needs for distribution to local organizations

Exhibit No. 40

Hell, my name is _____. I work for A. Jay Cooper who is a
candidate for Mayor of Prichard in the run-off election on Sept.
12th. I would like to urge you as strongly as I can to please
vote on September 12th for Jay Cooper.

if you need a ride to the polls, we will provide you with
transportation. (get number from them or give 456-3371).

Would you be able to help us in the campaign now?
If you have any teenagers or know of any who would be willing to
help after school to distribute literature, it would be extremely
helpful to us. They should report to our campaign office
926 St. Stephens Rd.

We also need urgently drivers on election day; can you
volunteer to drive for us.

Phone bank conversation format

113

COOPER CAMPAIGN

TELEPHONE BANK VOLUNTEER FORM

NAME_____

ADDRESS_____TEL._____

VOLUNTEER POSITIONS

POLL WORKERS_____

POLL WATCHERS_____ (Tuesday August 8th only)

DAY CARE_____

DRIVER_____ Do you have a car?_____

CANVASSER_____ Do you have a car?_____

PHONE BANK_____

HEADQUARTERS STAFF_____ A. Typist_____

                                           B. Receptionist_____

                                           C. Tel Operator_____

                                           D. Mimeo Oper. _____

                                           E. Office aid_____

                                           Dispatchers

                                           for Headquarters_____

What hours would you be available to work?_____

Sample..... 8 to 3 ( )

          3 to 7 ( )

          7 to 11 ( )

How soon can you start to work?_____

Do you have transportation to the office?_____

Phone bank volunteer form

Exhibit No. 42

DISTRIBUTION SCHEDULE FOR NEW LITERATURE BETWEEN SEPTEMBER 4TH AND 11TH

SEPTEMBER 4TH

1. Districts II, III, VI, and half of V (from Main to Station and I-65 over to Rich)

   Will be canvassed with 3,000 pieces of literature C. Around 50 people will be needed to accomplish this.

2. 300 bumper stickers will be given out in the morning at the major shopping centers, and in the afternoon at Spring Lake, Fostina, Chestang, and Edgewater Beaches.

3. Find 100 cars to put two posters on them for Labor Day...and beyond. Especially those cars going to Spring Lake, Fostina, Chestang and Edgewater Beaches. (200 posters needed)

4. Four people needed in the morning to canvas Prichard Shopping Center on Wilson Avenue. Each having 100 pieces of literature C.

5. Two people should cover each of the following intersections between 8:30 a.m. and 11:30 a.m., plus 6:30 p.m. and 8:30 p.m.

Wilson Ave. and Whistler Ave.	200 pieces literature C
St. Stephens Rd. and Clark St.	" " " "
St. Stephens Rd. and Prichard Ave.	" " " "
Wilson Ave. and St. Stephens Rd.	" " " "
Wilson Ave. and Prichard Ave.	" " " "

SEPTEMBER 5TH

1. Districts IV, VII, VIII, IX, X and remainder of V (Station, north into IV) will be canvassed with 300 pieces of literature C, 3,000 B in VII and VIII.

2. Around 30 people will be needed to accomplish this. Two hundred bumper stickers will be given out at the major shopping centers. Around 10 people will be needed to carry this out.

3. 250 black business window posters.

SEPTEMBER 6TH   Above Station into IV between I-65 and Rich

1. Districts I, IV, V, IX, will be canvassed with 4,000 pieces of literature B. Attempt to recruit as many white supporters as possible. Need approximately 20 to 30 people.

2. Major shopping centers - 600 pieces literature C.

3. 250 poster distribution on black community streets, 250 poster distribution on white community streets.

Literature distribution plan and schedule

115

SEPTEMBER 7TH

1. Districts II, III, V, VI, VII, VIII, IX, and X will be canvassed with 4,000
   pieces of literature D. Will need around 30 to 40 people to carry this out.

2. 200 bumper stickers to be given out in the major shopping centers of Prichard.

3. Two people should be at each of the following intersections between 5:00 p.m.
   and 8:00 p.m.--

   1) Wilson Ave. and Whistler Ave.
   2) St. Stephens Rd. and Clark Street
   3) St. Stephens and Prichard Ave.
   4) Wilson Ave. and St. Stephens Rd.
   5) Wilson Ave. and Prichard Ave.

SEPTEMBER 8TH

1. Districts I, II, III, IV, V, VI, VII, IX, X, Ward 5 and 6 have been disignated
   to be canvassed with 5,000 pieces of literature C.

2. Districts I, IV, VII, and X, will be canvassed with 5,000 pieces of literature D.

3. 200 bumper stickers should be given out at the below-listed intersections:

   1) St. Stephens Rd. and Wilson Ave.
   2) Stone St. and Wilson Ave. (on Stone St.)
   3) Prichard Ave. and St. Stephens Rd.

   These bumper stickers will be distributed between the hours of 7:00 a.m. and
   8:30 a.m., plus between 3:00 p.m. and 6:00 p.m.

4. We will need at least twelve (12) people to carry this out effectively.
   Shopping center - 1000, lapel stickers - 500 in white community.

SEPTEMBER 9TH

1. Districts II, III, IV, VI, VII, and VIII will be canvassed with 4,000 pieces
   of literature A (2,000) in districts II, III, IV, VI. Literature B (3,000)
   pieces will be distributed in districts VI and VIII. Around 30-40 people
   will be needed to carry this out.

2. Intersections should be covered by (on) September 9th:

   1) Wilson Ave. and Whistler Ave.
   2) St. Stephens Rd. and Clarke St.
   3) St. Stephens and Prichard Ave.
   4) Wilson Ave. and St. Stephens
   5) Wilson Ave. and Prichard Ave.
   6) Stone Street and Wilson Ave. (on Stone St.)

   Around 24 people are needed for this. 400 bumper stickers will be distributed. Literature A, B, C, D, will be used. As close to fifty (50) of each
   as possible. Time of distribution: 9:00 a.m. to 1:00 p.m., plus 4:00 p.m.
   to 8:30 p.m..

116

3. All the major shopping centers should be canvassed. Around 15 to 20 people are needed to carry this out.

SEPTEMBER 10TH

1. Canvass all the black churces, using literature A

2. 300 bumper stickers to be distributed at B. Stress church-going young people to carry this out.

SEPTEMBER 11TH

1. Districts I, II, III, IV, V, VI, VII, VIII, IX, and X. The remaining pieces of literature A and B will be used to make a complete sweep of the city. Districts VII, VIII, IX and X will get the remainder of literature B. Districts I, III, IV, V, and IX will get the remainder of literature A.

2. The remainder of the bumper stickers will be distributed at the major shopping centers during the day.

3. 5,000 door knob hangers will be distributed in Districts I, II, III IV, V, VI VIII, and IX, beginning at dusk or 8:00 p.m. for the entire day. Will need 200 people.

SAVE PRICHARD

VOTE THIS SAMPLE
BALLOT ON SEPT. 12th

MAYOR
( ) Vernon O. Capps
(X) A."Jay" Cooper

PLACE #1
(X) Handy L. Davis
( ) Edward "Joe" Graham

PLACE #2
(X) Freddie L.(Fred) Harris
( ) Larry Sullivan

PLACE #3
( ) L.J. Keen
(X) John Langham

PLACE #4
( ) W. Leonard Mosely
(X) Shafter Summers

PLACE #5
( ) Alford W. Turner
(X) Don Lyons

Endorsed & Recommendation
of the Baptist Ministers
Conference of Prichard
Progressive Organized Workers
of Prichard

Paid Political Advertising by
Citizens for Prichard

Sample ballot, handbill

SAMPLE BALLOT
RUN-OFF SEPT. 12

MAYOR
( ) Vernon O. Capps
(★) A. J. 'JAY' COOPER

PLACE 1
(★) Handy L. Davis
( ) Edward "Joe" Graham

PLACE 2
(★) Freddie L. (Fred) Harris
( ) Larry Sullivan

PLACE 3
( ) L. J. Keen
(★) John Langham

PLACE 4
( ) W. Leonard Moseley
(★) Shafter Summers

PLACE 5
( ) Alford W. Turner
(★) Don Lyons

Paid Pol. Adv.

Sample ballot, door knob hanger

Together - We Can
SAVE PRICHARD
Vote Sept. 12 For COOPER
And Keep Prichard From
Bankruptcy

Pd. Pol Adv. By A.J. Cooper

A.J. "JAY" COOPER

POLL WATCHER REPORT

WARD NUMBER _____

MACHINE NUMBER _____

BOX NUMBER _____

KEY NUMBER _____

PROTECTIVE COUNTER NUMBER (1) _____

PUBLIC COUNTER NUMBER (1) _____

PROTECTIVE COUNTER NUMBER (2) _____

PUBLIC COUNTER NUMBER (2) _____

ESTIMATED VOTE PER HOUR

10:00 11:00 12:00 1:00 2:00 3:00 4:00 5:00 6:00

COOPER

CAPPS

Poll Watchers record the above information from the tally sheet when your machine is closed. Give to COOPER CHIEF WATCHER. Chief Poll Watchers must use this form to record and report the final total of all votes cast in the ward for our candidate. The total of all machines for each candidate should be added and placed in the appropriate box above. Your totals must equal the total recorded by the official ward tally sheet.
DO NOT LEAVE THE POLLING PLACE UNTIL YOU ARE SURE ALL TOTALS ARE ACCURATE AND MACHINES ARE PROPERLY LOCKED. (Be sure to count challenged ballots.)

CALL HEADQUARTERS: 457-7011 or 456-1475 WITH PROBLEMS

Vote tally sheet (one prepared for each voting machine)

HOW TO REGISTER TO VOTE

In order to register to vote you must go to the Mobile County Court House on South Royal Street at Government Street. Go into the Board of Registrars office. This office will be open six (6) Days a week, beginning Saturday, August 19, 1972 for the registration of eligible voters. If you cannot read or write request the clerk to fill out the registration form.

REGISTRATION HOURS

Monday thur Firday	9:00 a.m. till 4:30 p.m.
Saturday	8:30 a.m. till 11:00 a.m.

IDENTIFICATION AND REFERENCES

IDENTIFICATION: EXAMPLES
Birth Certificate
Driver's Licsence
Medicare Card

REFERENCE On paper take with you the names, addresses, and Telephone numbers of two (2) persons who know that you have live in your hame for 30 days or more.

REGISTRATION PROBLEMS

If for some reason the clerk refuses to register you as a voter, have the clerk put into writing the reasons you cannot become a registered voter, then have the clerk to sign the statement. If the clerk will not write down the reasons why you cannot register, take the clerk's name and call 456-1475.
After you recieve the signed statement, Please call 456-1475, so that the proper action may be taken to solve the problem.

After you become a registered voter you may find out what ward to votw in on September 12th, by looking on the third (3rd) line on the left side of the certificate of registration given to you at the registrars office.

VOTING FOR THE FIRST TIME SEPTEMBER 12th

You may have to vote on what is called a paper challenge ballot and your registration slip may need to be attached to the paper challenge ballot for proof that you are a registered voter.

For any additional information please call 456-1475.
Do not fail to call if you have any questions that need answering.

Voter registration instruction sheet

Exhibit No. 47

PEOPLE UNITED FOR ACTION VOTER REGISTRATION SURVEY

NAME _____

ADDRESS _____

TELEPHONE _____ AGE _____

ARE YOU A REGISTERED VOTER? YES( ) NO( )

IF YOU REGISTERED SOMEWHERE ELSE BEFORE MOVING TO PRICHARD, DID YOU
NOTIFY THE BOARD OF REGISTRARS OF YOUR CHANGE OF ADDRESS? YES( ) NO( )

NUMBER OF PERSONS LIVING IN HOUSEHOLD

    18 AND Under ( )
    18 to 30   ( )
    30 and Over   ( )

Voter registration canvass sheet

123

```
                          STAFF MEETING
                            8-22-72


FUND RAISING

        I. Gospel Sing

              1. Letters of notification will be mailed 8-22-72
              2. Plans and recommendations for August 28.

                    a. use of ministers in program
                    b. use of volunteers around city
                    c. open door program
                    d. donations at door dismissed - collection table agreed on
                    e. notification of all churches

       II. Cabaret

              1. Held at the Harlem Club
              2. Door prizes
              3. Odyssey Four - band
              4. Radio announcements

      III. Beauty Contest

              1. Mardi Gras - September 3
              2. Tickets - optional
              3. Entertainment

                    a. fashion show - Models-a-la-Mode
                    b. music - Odyssey Four
                    c. beauty contest

              4. Advertisement

                    a. Mobile Beacon
                    b. radio - public service spots
                    c. Mardi Gras announcer
                    d. Jay will talk to Douglas about use of kitchen
                    e. prizes - undecided

VOTER REGISTRATION

        I. Hard count for 8-22-72

       II. 179 total count

      III. There is a need for finding the total percentage of blacks who
           register to vote

       IV. Drivers

              1. 13 present for Sat., 8-19
              2. 5 present for Mon., 8-21
              3. 7 present for Tues., 8-22
```

Minutes of staff meeting outlining voter registration strategies

   V. Number of people at phone bank

      1. 12 present
      2. 4 on phones at all times

  VI. Suggestion - request help from 100 Women for Cooper

 VII. Recommendation - push up voter registration to 100 per day

VIII. Problem - mis-information on cards

  IX. Means of increasing voter registration

      1. 100 women to canvas neighborhoods
      2. Minister Radio Show - send a letter requesting the announcement
         on Wed., and give a follow-up call on Fri.
      3. Request radio public service spots
      4. Notify any meeting organization
      5. Notify ladies' service clubs for help
      6. Address letters to churches not ministers
      7. Signs offering rides to register on cars
      8. Have influential people assign meeting post
      9. 18-25 year old voters will be given a rally and an all-day
         record hop
     10. Give all ideas to Ann

   X. Headquarters I

      1. Meeting on 8-23
      2. Need a distribution schedule for old and new material
      3. Marching orders will be given

Exhibit No. 49

```
┌─────────────────────────────────────────────────────────────────────┐
```

INSTRUCTIONS FOR GETTING AND FILLING OUT AN APPLICATION
FOR AN ABSENTEE BALLOT BY MAIL

I.   How to get an application for an Absentee Ballot

     Any registered voter who will be absent from Prichard, or unable

     to go to his polling place on the date of the election, is

     eligible to vote by Absentee Ballot. In order to get an Absentee

     Ballot you must first get an "Application for Absentee Ballot

     by mail." Any person may get this form from Bernice H. Centanne,

     City Clerk, of the City of Prichard, Alabama, at her office in the

     City Hall. Any representative of anyone desiring an Absentee

     Ballot, such as a parent, member of the family, etc, may also

     get an application for an Absentee Ballot Form for a registered

     voter by identifying himself and the person for whom he wishes to

     get the application, at the City Clerks Office.

     The Application for an Absentee Ballot Form must be filled out as

     indicated below and sent back to the City Clerk by registered

     mail. The City Clerk then mails an absentee ballot to the person

     who should fill it in immediately and send it back by registered

     mail to the address that will be indicated. A registered voter

     has until September 6th, to send in his application for an

     Absentee Ballot Form. Once he receives his absentee ballot, he

     should mail it so that it reaches City Hall before September 12.

II.
     How to Complete the Application for an Absentee Ballot

     A. Fill in the date that you complete the Absentee application.

     B. Print your name and ward number.

     C. Give your full birthdate.

     D. Give your full street address in the city of Prichard.

     E. Print "Prichard Run-Off Election" to be held on the 12th day
         of September, 1972.

     F. Check the appropriate reason that you will be unable to go to
         the polling place on the day of the election.
         1. In the event that you are a university or college student,
             give the full name of the institution which you are
             attending.

         2. If you are disabled, give the place or institution where
             you are confined.

     G. On the three blank lines, print the name and the address at
         which you wish the Absentee Ballot to be mailed complete with
         zip code.

     H. Sign the application.

III. Completion of the portion of the Application which covers members

     of the armed forces or wives of members of the armed forces,

     disabled veterans or students.

Absentee ballot instruction sheet

126

A. Have your name filled in after the words "The above applicant". After the words "was identified properly and this application was signed in the presence of", print the name of either your commanding officer, chief of medical services, registrar, or assistant registrar (of the college or university you are attending). Put your name after the words "I certify that."

B. Have the application signed as provided for.

IV. Physically disabled applicants

If you are physically disabled, you are to fill out the third portion by filling in the name of a practicing physician in the first line, your name following the word "applicant" and the name of the institution or place where you are confined and the reason for your confinement. Have your doctor sign the application before a notary public, and have the notary public sign also.

V. Have this application mailed to the following address"

Berniece H. Centanne, City Clerk, Prichard, Alabama 36610.

VI. It is recommended that this application form and the Absentee Ballot itself be mailed by registered mail.

.... Also drop a note to A."Jay" Cooper for Mayor Campaign, Headquarters Number 3 , 553 South Wilson Ave. Prichard, Alabama 36610, to let us know when you mailed your application form back, and when you mailed your Absentee Ballot back. This is Important.

Voting Machine Sample Ballot
Municipal Election, City of Prichard
September 12, 1972

DIRECTIONS FOR VOTING:

1. VOTER STEPS INTO THE BOOTH.
   (Curtains are closed by the election officers)
2. TURN POINTERS OVER CANDIDATES OF YOUR CHOICE. (Let lever stay in down position)
3. PRESS DOWN RED BUTTON TO RECORD YOUR VOTE. (Located to your left)

1	2	3	4	5	6	7	8	9	10	11	12

| FOR MAYOR (Vote for One) | | FOR COUNCILMAN, PLACE 1 (Vote for One) | | FOR COUNCILMAN, PLACE 2 (Vote for One) | | FOR COUNCILMAN, PLACE 3 (Vote for One) | | FOR COUNCILMAN, PLACE 4 (Vote for One) | | FOR COUNCILMAN, PLACE 5 (Vote for One) | |

| Vernon O. Capps | A"Jay" Cooper | Handy L. Davis | Edward J. Graham | Fred L. Harris | Larry Sullivan | L. J. Keen | John Lanahan | "J.Leonard Shafter | "oseley Summers | Don Lyons | Alford Turner |

PRESS THIS RED BUTTON AFTER YOU HAVE PULLED THE LEVERS OVER THE NAMES OF THE CANDIDATES YOU WISH TO VOTE FOR. MAKE SURE THAT YOU DO NOT MOVE LEVERS ONCE YOU PUSH THE DOWN.

IF YOU MOVE THE LEVERS BACK TO THEIR ORIGINAL POSITION YOU WILL ERASE YOUR VOTE.

Voting machine ballot diagram for voter education program

128

Voter Education Stations are ar the following churches:

Good Will, Antioch Baptist, Cedar Grove, Mount Sinai, Mt.
Carmel and St. James Catholic Church.

We will have a person at each church to enlain how to use
the voting machine. It is most important that each new
Voter come to one of these churches tomorrow before going to
the Polls if possible, if not please call 456-3371 for this
information on the phone.

Sponsored by the P.O.W.

Radio spot announcing voter education program